The Invisible Minority

GLBTQ Youth At Risk, 2nd Edition

By

Bob Latham

authorHOUSE™

1663 LIBERTY DRIVE, SUITE 200
BLOOMINGTON, INDIANA 47403
(800) 839-8640
WWW.AUTHORHOUSE.COM

First published by AuthorHouse 06/21/05

ISBN: 1-4208-5328-7 (sc)

Printed in the United States of America
Bloomington, Indiana

This book is printed on acid-free paper.

DEDICATION

This book is dedicated to Stanley Alan Cornfield
who was my best friend and lover
for 15 wonderful years.
He still inspires.

TABLE OF CONTENTS

FOREWORD

The United States prides itself in being a democratic society with strong traditions of justice for all. Civil and human rights are basic tenets of American life. We are proud that the Bill of Rights in our Constitution has established freedoms unknown in many other parts of the world. And many of us have worked very hard to ensure that our rights and freedoms extend to groups, which have historically been the victims of discrimination and prejudice, particularly on the basis of religion, race, ethnic identity, and sex. We understand that the protection of the rights of any one of us depends on protection of the rights of all of us.

We also pride ourselves on our diversity. Even when rights and opportunities are not applied equally, we recognize that the active participation and contributions of individuals of many different groups -- racial and ethnic, religious, male and female, social and cultural, of all ages -- make our society more vital, productive, and satisfying. We know that if any of us is vilified, scapegoated, or made the subject of violence or discrimination because of his or her group identity, none of us is safe.

Discrimination and stereotypes based on sexual orientation have been among the most difficult human rights issues for many to acknowledge. Despite civil rights gains in other areas, gay, lesbian, bisexual, and transgender people still face major problems. Adults continue to face discrimination, particularly in jobs and housing. Students and adults alike face name-calling, taunting, hatred, and physical violence. Few, and particularly the young, have access to sympathetic support and guidance. Most young people in this minority group do not have family members who can help them cope. If homophobia continues unchecked and uninterrupted in the classroom or in the community, a message is sent that scapegoating and targeting is okay.

Gay teenagers are two to three times more likely to attempt suicide. Prejudice leads to harassment, ostracism, and, all too frequently, violence against them. These young people experience high rates of AIDS and other sexually transmitted diseases, drug abuse, dropping out of school, and running away from home. Their very existence is generally ignored or even denied. Additionally, there are students who have a gay or lesbian parent, brother or sister, or other close relative. It is important that these students get the message that they are okay and that their family is valued and accepted. All children are entitled to protection, to honest information about all aspects of their lives, and to equal access to counseling, support, and educational opportunities. Educators committed to justice and human rights need to continue to examine their own responsibilities. There are students in almost every classroom who are or will be gay or lesbian. They need support and protection -- and the opportunity to mature into sensitive, confident, productive adults regardless of their sexual orientation.

This Foreword was adapted from *Affording Equal Opportunity to Gay and Lesbian Students Through Teaching and Counseling* by the National Education Association.

ACKNOWLEDGMENTS

This book is an outgrowth of the Mentor Project that I did for West Contra Costa Unified School District in 1992. The Mentor Report was distributed within the district in 1993. A special thanks to Anna Blackman, who was my supervisor for the Mentor Project and who later became Deputy Superintendent.

Since 1993 I have done many workshops for high school students and faculty and administrators at all levels, preschool through college. The approach has been widely used with great success by Grant Peterson especially in Alameda County, California using United Way grants. His work began as part of BANGLE (Bay Area Network of Gay and Lesbian Educators). BANGLE is now the San Francisco-East Bay Chapter of GLSEN (Gay, Lesbian and Straight Education Network) and workshops on sexual orientation are a major focus.

Many new resources have become available in the last several years. This book incorporates new information and hopefully will be of use beyond the San Francisco Bay Area.

Material and advice from the groups, individuals, and publications listed below have been used both directly and indirectly. Many thanks to all.

Affording Equal Opportunity to Gay and Lesbian Students Through Teaching and Counseling (A Training Handbook for Educators) National Education Association

Bay Area Network of Gay and Lesbian Educators (BANGLE), East Bay Chapter and Contra Costa County Chapter

Building Bridges, Exploring the Needs of the Gay Community (A Training Guide) United Way of the Bay Area

Equity Institute Inc./Project Empowerment (No longer active.)

GLSEN (Gay, Lesbian and Straight Education Network)
121 West 27th Street, Suite 804, New York, NY 10001

Pacific Center for Human Growth
2712 Telegraph Avenue, Berkeley, CA 94705

The P.E.R.S.O.N. Project (Public Education Regarding Sexual Orientation Nationally), Jean Richter--richter@eecs.berkeley.edu
Web page at: http://www.youth.org/loco/PERSONProject/

Project 10 Handbook, Virginia Uribe, PhD
7850 Melrose Avenue, Los Angeles, CA 90046

United Teachers of Richmond Gay and Lesbian Caucus
3065 Richmond Parkway, Suite 101, Richmond, CA 94806

HINTS ON USING THIS BOOK

This book is designed to be "user friendly," to provide easy access to parts that will be useful to you. You are hereby granted permission to copy pages for presentations in classrooms and to faculty, administration, and community groups. Page breaks and font size have sometimes been manipulated to facilitate copying. For example, the font size of the vocabulary list on page 2 is small so that all the words fit on one page.

If you don't have time to read the entire book, please read the first ten pages for basic information and then consult the Table of Contents for parts that will be most useful to you.

The Appendixes contain excellent information, so please do not overlook them.

An attempt has been made to include recent print, video, and website resources. Of course changes occur rapidly, especially in websites. Therefore, doing a website search for more recent resources is always a good idea in this century. If you have any corrections or suggested additions, I would appreciate receiving them. The website www.Q-zine.com has my current contact information.

National GLSEN (Gay, Lesbian and Straight Education Network) provides a particularly valuable website that includes information on new resources as they are developed. The address is www.glsen.org.

INTRODUCTION

Why is special help needed for gay, lesbian, bisexual, transgender, and questioning (GLBTQ) youth in our schools?

Some of the more important reasons are the following:

1 This minority continues to face extreme persecution.

2. Members of this minority usually do not have family members who can help them cope.

3. Nearly one third of all teen age suicides are related to persecution around the issue of sexual orientation and gender identity.

3. Every classroom contains one or more students who now or will eventually identify themselves as gay or lesbian.

Information about gay, lesbian, bisexual, and transgender people will help all students. Many students who are heterosexual go through a period of anxiety when wondering about their own sexual orientation. If homosexuality is demystified it will be less of a concern to everyone, including heterosexual students. Also, many heterosexual students have family members or friends who are GLBT.

The demystification of homosexuality will also reduce sexism. Homophobia is often a driving force in sexist behavior.

For facts and statistics on GLBT students and schools, see Appendix 3.

(This book is designed with page breaks to facilitate copying various pages for classroom or other presentation use. The next five pages are meant to be copied for presentations, the quiz used separately from the rest.)

VOCABULARY

Homosexual: A person who is emotionally, physically, and/or sexually attracted or committed to members of the same sex.

Heterosexual: A person who is emotionally, physically, and/or sexually attracted or committed to members of the other sex.

Gay: A common and acceptable word for male homosexuals, but also used for males and females together. More recently "queer" or GLBT (Gay, Lesbian, Bisexual, Transgender) is used to emphasize inclusion.

Lesbian: A common and acceptable word for female homosexuals only.

Bisexual: A person who is emotionally, physically, and/or sexually attracted to both sexes.

Racism: The irrational fear of members of a different race. Often based on a belief in false stereotypes.

Homophobia: The irrational fear of homosexuals or homosexuality. Often based on a belief in false stereotypes.

Heterosexism: The assumption that everyone is and should be heterosexual.

Coming out: To "come out" is to publicly declare and affirm one's GLBT identity, sometimes to one person in conversation, sometimes by an act that places one in the public eye. It is not a single event but instead a life-long process. In many new situations a GLBT person must decide whether or not to come out.

In the closet: Means to hide one's GLBT identity in order to keep a job, a housing situation, friends, etc. Many GLBT people are "out" in some situations and "closeted" in others.

Transvestite: Men and women who enjoy wearing the clothes of and appearing as the other sex. Most are heterosexual.

Transsexual: Men and women who feel they have the wrong set of sexual organs. Many transsexuals have sex-change operations. There is no connection between transsexuality and homosexuality.

Transgender: A general term that includes transvestites, transsexuals, and people born with ambiguous or dual sexual organs.

Civil/Human Rights: Equal treatment of all people with respect to life, liberty, and property and to the protection of law. This includes jobs, housing, and family units.

Tolerance: The acceptance of differences in people; lack of prejudice and harassment.

A QUIZ ON GAY AND LESBIAN ISSUES

Read each statement below and fill in the blank: "T" for true or "F" for false. Just put the first answer that comes to mind, don't worry too much about whether or not it is right or wrong.

_____ 1. Lesbian/gay people can ordinarily be identified by certain mannerisms or physical characteristics.

_____ 2. Homosexual behavior is found only in humans (not animals).

_____ 3. We know what causes homosexuality.

_____ 4. Most lesbian/gay people can be cured by having really good sex with a member of the opposite sex.

_____ 5. The majority of child molesters are lesbian/gay.

_____ 6. Lesbian/gay people should not be teachers or parents because they will try to convert young people into the gay lifestyle.

_____ 7. Lesbian/gay people have made a conscious decision to be that way.

_____ 8. Gay/lesbian parents raise gay/lesbian children.

_____ 9. Homosexuality is a type of mental illness and can be cured by appropriate psychotherapy.

_____ 10. One homosexual experience as an adolescent will play a large part in determining whether a person will be homosexually oriented as an adult.

(Answers on page 6)

Write one or more questions you would like answered about GLBT people below:

_____

_____

_____

_____

BACKGROUND

Homosexuality is a normal variation that occurs in nature in many species and among most, if not all, of humankind's various cultures. Homosexuality is a variation very much like left-handedness. Most of the population is right-handed. A significant minority of the population is naturally left-handed. Left-handed people are present in all occupations and have made important contributions throughout history. Similarly, most of the population is heterosexual. A significant minority of the population is naturally homosexual. Homosexual people are present in all occupations and have made important contributions throughout history (see the next page and consider posting it).

The causes of sexual orientation, whether heterosexual or homosexual, are not established and are probably quite complex. Recent research indicates that there *may* be differences in parts of the brain and in the genetic makeup between the two groups. These studies indicate that sexual orientation is already determined at birth. That conclusion is speculative, and not particularly relevant to what needs to be done in schools now. What is relevant (and well established by many studies and expert testimony in court) is the fact that sexual orientation is established by the time that a child reaches school age. This means that education about homosexuality in schools will not create homosexuals, but may allow everyone to reach their natural orientation with less pain and suffering.

Extensive research over the last 50 years indicate that about 10% of the population in the United States is exclusively homosexual. Kinsey's research indicates that an additional 5% engage in homosexual behavior part of the time. These numbers have been confirmed by many other scientists for the United States as well as in other cultures, but some recent research obtained lower percentages. Even if the percent is much smaller, it does not change what needs to be done in schools to meet the needs of our invisible minority.

Some people have difficulty with homosexuality due to religious beliefs. It is important to realize that spirituality is an important part of the lives of most GLBT people. It may be useful to study "Homosexuality and the Bible: What you really need to know" (Appendix 1).

GAY MEN AND WOMEN WHO ENRICHED THE WORLD

By Thomas Cowan, Alyson Publications, Inc. 1992.

**Short Biographies
including evidence of sexual orientation
are included on the following people:**

Alexander the Great	Plato
Sappho	Leonardo da Vinci
Desiderius Erasmus	Michelangelo
Francis Bacon	Christopher Marlowe
Frederick the Great	Madame de Stael
Lord Byron	Herman Melville
Walt Whitman	Horatio Alger, Jr.
Oscar Wilde	Tchaikovsky
Marcel Proust	Willa Cather
Colette	Amy Lowell
Gertrude Stein	E.M. Forster
Virginia Woolf	John M. Keynes
T.E. Lawrence	Ludwig Wittgenstein
Jean Cocteau	Bessie Smith
Charles Laughton	Noel Coward
Marguerite Yourcenar	Christopher Isherwood
Tennessee Williams	Alan Turing
Benjamin Britten	Pier Paolo Pasolini
James Baldwin	Yukio Mishima
Andy Warhol	Michael Bennett

WHAT EVERYONE SHOULD KNOW ABOUT HOMOSEXUALITY

1. Nobody knows what causes heterosexuality or homosexuality. There is probably no single factor.

2. Sexual orientation appears to be established early in life.

3. Attempts to change homosexuals into heterosexuals have been largely unsuccessful.

4. Most homosexuals are unidentifiable by appearance or mannerism.

5. Homosexuality is NOT a mental illness. It was declassified as such by the American Psychiatric Association in 1973.

6. Homosexuals are NOT sick, deviant or perverted.

7. Homosexuals have the same capacity for loving, long lasting relationships and productive lives as do heterosexuals.

(All 10 of the quiz questions on page 3 were false--they are common misconceptions.)

WHAT ALL TEACHERS AND STAFF SHOULD DO

1. **Do not let sexual orientation slurs go unchallenged.** This is extremely important. It is the most common request that I received in talking to groups of young GLBT people. A sexual orientation slur should be treated the same as a racial slur. Slurs of all types should not be tolerated in the classroom, hallways, school grounds, or faculty rooms.

Slurs are frequently made with naiveté and ignorance. A gentle comment like "The statement you just made is offensive to me." followed by a bit of education as to why it is offensive, usually works best. This line is particularly effective when you are not a member of the slurred group. See Appendix 2 for more on this topic.

2. **Include sexual orientation whenever diversity tolerance units are presented.** This request was given highest priority by the youth groups I surveyed. In fact, sexual orientation should be included whenever diversity or tolerance issues are *raised*. At this point in history in the United States, the level of discrimination against lesbian, gay, bisexual, and transgender people is probably greater than for any other minority.

3. **Make information on gay hot lines, websites, groups, etc. available to all students.** This request was also given highest priority by the youth groups I surveyed. On page 21 is an example of Youth Resources suitable for posting and distribution in the San Francisco Bay Area. It includes national resources but needs to be modified to include local resources for other geographic areas.

CLASSES THAT TEACH SEXUALITY

(BIOLOGY, CHILD DEVELOPMENT, HEALTH, PHYSIOLOGY, PSYCHOLOGY, SOCIOLOGY, etc.)

Because many students have relatives or friends who are lesbian, gay, bisexual, or transgender and because many other students are wondering about their own sexual orientation, it is extremely important that homosexuality be covered in a non-judgmental, matter-of-fact way whenever sexuality is studied. Most textbooks do not have an adequate treatment of homosexuality. The following is a suggested plan for a three-day unit to provide the minimum information that should be included. (You will need **class set copies of pages 2, 3, 4, 5, 6, and 21** from this book, pages 2 and 3 separate from the others and page 21 modified as necessary for geographic location.)

Depending on your school policy you may need to use a parent permission slip before doing this unit. The first presentations I did in my own high school chemistry classes did not have parent permission slips and garnered some parent complaints. After that, I used parent permission slips that provided an alternative student activity in the library. With the permission slips, there were no parent complaints and very few students chose to avoid the sexual orientation unit. See page 11 for the Parent Permission that I used. Notice that it had to be returned ONLY if the student was NOT to participate in the unit.

Day 1 With only a brief introduction, distribute and discuss the vocabulary list (page 2 of this book.) Then distribute "A Quiz on Gay and Lesbian Issues", page 3. (The quiz includes a request for a question the student would like answered.) After about 10 minutes, collect the quiz papers so that what was written remains anonymous. Announce that all 10 of the quiz question are false. They are common misconceptions. Discuss the quiz questions as needed (see Appendix 4, pages 38-41 for suggestions). Make a short presentation of the material contained on pages 4 and 42 of this book. Distribute copies of pages 4, 5, 6, and 21 ("Background," "Gay Men and Women who Enriched the World," "What Everyone Should Know about Homosexuality," and "Youth Resources" which has been modified as needed for your geographic area.) The rest of the period can be used for discussion, writing, and/or reading the handouts.

Day 2 Show the video "Gay Youth" (See Appendix 11). After the 40-minute video, use the rest of the period for discussion or a writing assignment such as "Make a list of what you learned from the video."

Day 3 Panel of speakers. (See Educational Resources, page 20. Make arrangements for speakers well in advance. If they are available, panelists who are recent alumni or current students in the school are particularly effective.) Summarize some of the student questions for the speakers and/or read some of the questions during the session if you need help in answering them.

Make optional assignments if desired (see suggestions below).

Optional Assignments.

1. The Background page said that homosexuality is a "normal variation that occurs in nature in many species." Do a library search to find at least five animal species in which homosexual behavior has been observed. Write a report summarizing this information and documenting the references.

2. The Background page said that homosexuality is found "among most, if not all, of mankind's various cultures." Do a library search to find information on homosexuality in at least three cultures other than the United States. Write a report summarizing this information and documenting the references.

3. Summarize the biography of one of the 40 people listed in *Gay Men and Women who Enriched the World*. Look up the same person in three or more other sources. Do any of these other sources give information about sexual orientation?

4. Imagine that you are the parent of a teenager who has just told you that she or he is gay. What is your response? Suggestion: Try writing the exchange as a scene in a play.

5. The discrimination and persecution that gays face is sometimes compared to that based on race or religion at various points in history. Pick some specific area of persecution and discrimination in history and compare and contrast that to the persecution and discrimination faced by gays today.

6. Enter the current GLSEN (Gay, Lesbian and Straight Education Network) essay or writing contest if there is one in your area.

7. Make a list of countries where gay marriage is legal. Include states or provinces if appropriate. Include information on results if available.

8. Make a list of countries that include homosexual people in their military forces. Include information on results if available.

9. Do some research and write a report on intersexuals.

10. Do some research and write a report about cross dressers, people who are heterosexual, have no interest in changing their gender, but enjoy dressing as a member of the opposite sex.

Sample Parent Permission Letter:

SCHOOL LETTERHEAD

Dear Student and Parent or Guardian:

I personally feel that tolerance and appreciation of diversity is worthwhile and beneficial. It is also the policy of this school district. Diversity includes people of different races, different religions, different mental and physical abilities, and different sexual orientations to name a few.

In an effort to promote tolerance and reduce harassment at this school, I plan to do a short unit in this class from the book titled *The Invisible Minority: GLBTQ Youth At Risk*. The unit will include showing the video titled "Gay Youth" which has been extensively reviewed and approved for viewing by high school students in this district.

The unit will be scheduled to minimize loss of class time and will not appreciably affect the amount of other material covered in this class. Total time spent on the unit will be about 80 minutes.

An alternative written assignment will be provided in a different room for those students who do not want to participate in this unit. If the alternative assignment is chosen, please sign and return the form below.

Sincerely yours,

Robert R. Latham   Doreen Covell
Chemistry & Physics Teacher   Principal

I do not want my student, _____ ,

to participate in the tolerance and diversity unit.

                                                    _____

                                                    Signed by Parent or Guardian

ENGLISH CLASSES

English teachers have a unique opportunity to help students develop a better understanding of sexual orientation. The choice of literature, writing assignments, and even vocabulary words can he helpful in this area. It is appropriate and important to mention the sexual orientation of GLBT authors because heterosexism is pervasive in our society. When I was in high school, it would have helped me a great deal to know that some of the authors I was reading were gay or lesbian or bisexual.

If sexual orientation comes up in the classroom, it may be desirable to do the unit outlined in the previous section, Classes that Teach Sexuality. The Optional Assignments are all appropriate for English classes.

In choosing literature to be covered, it is reasonable to include at least one book each year that has lesbian or gay characters. Some of the better books that I have found include the following:

Trying Hard to Hear You by Sandra Scoppettone (Alyson Publications, Inc., Boston, 1991.) This is an excellent novel that I found difficult to put down. The story is set in a close-knit teenage summer theater group. Unusual depth and complex plot threads in a contemporary teenage setting makes this a worthwhile and popular choice for a high school English class. The fact that two members of the group are gay is not disclosed until the second half of the book. First person narration is by a straight sixteen-year-old. Sexual orientation is only one of many facets of the story.

Fried Green Tomatoes/Whistle Stop Cafe by Fannie Flagg (McGraw-Hill, Inc., New York, 1988.) This is an excellent novel that was a best seller and which was made into an academy award caliber movie (Jessica Tandy was nominated for best supporting actress.) The book incorporates an interesting style of writing. It has many short chapters set in different time periods. The Lesbian relationship is more developed in the book than in the movie. The relationship is presented in a low-key, tasteful manner.

Patience & Sarah by Isabel Miller (Fawcett Crest. New York. 1969.) This is a historical novel set in nineteenth century New England. It has a simple reading level and structure. The novel is a good choice to illustrate point of view in writing. The narration alternates between Patience and Sarah as their story unfolds. It was a Literary Guild selection. The book *Gay American History* by Jonathan Katz (Thomas Y. Crowell Company, New York, 1976) has an interesting interview with the author pages 433-443. The interview includes how the book came to be written and the difficulties in getting it published. (The interview is with Alma Routsong. Isabel Miller is a pen name.)

The Last of the Wine by Mary Renault (Pocket Books, Inc., New York, 1964.) This is an excellent historical novel set in ancient Greece during the wars between Athens and Sparta. Mary Renault brings the era alive while including many carefully researched historic facts including gay relationships. This novel is one of my personal favorites.

Billy's Boy by Patricia Nell Warren (Wildcat Press, Beverly Hills, 1997) is the third novel in the series that began with *The Front Runner*. The narrator in this novel is a teenage boy who searches for information about the mysterious death of his gay father and eventually learns that his mother is a lesbian. The novel covers all of the issues that GLBTQ youth sometimes face in schools and in society in an interesting way and should appeal to high school students.

Profiles in Gay & Lesbian Courage by Reverend Troy Perry (St. Martin's Press, New York, 1991) is an excellent non-fiction work. The stories of eight gay figures that showed bravery, dignity, and true courage are told in an engaging, even compelling way. Included are Harvey Milk, Elaine Noble, Gilberto Gerald, Jean O'Leary, Leonard Matlovich, Barbara Gittings, Harry Hay, and Ivy Bottini.

Appendix 12 contains additional titles that might be used. If you have other book suggestions or comments please send them to Bob Latham, P.O. Box 70554, Point Richmond, CA 94807 or by e-mail to BobLatham@aol.com.

HISTORY CLASSES

Many of the image and self-esteem problems faced by sexual orientation minorities are due to a feeling of isolation and lack of positive role models. Usually there is no one in the family who is a member of the same minority (unlike the situation for racial or ethnic minorities.) Too often harassment combines with low self-esteem and results in suicide. History teachers have an opportunity to make a significant difference in this area. Knowing that many of the people whose contributions are covered in history books were, in fact, gay would be a real benefit to all students.

It is important that the sexual orientation of historical figures be acknowledged in a matter-of-fact, low-keyed way. If sexual orientation becomes an issue, it may be desirable to do the unit outlined in the section, Classes that Teach Sexuality, pages 8-11. The Optional Assignments would also be appropriate for history classes.

Page 5 of this book should be copied and posted in your classroom. It lists the 40 people included in the book, *Gay Men and Women who Enriched the World* by Thomas Cowan. This book has short biographies and is recommended for student as well as teacher use.

Becoming Visible, A Reader in Gay & Lesbian History for High School & College Students, edited by Kevin Jennings, is an invaluable resource for history teachers. It includes information from the Greco-Roman world and ancient China to the present (1993). At the end of each chapter there is a list of outstanding questions and activities. The first chapter, "Understanding Heterosexism and Homophobia," is a concise and effective introduction that could be used alone.

Another book that is an excellent reference for history teachers is *Hidden from History: Reclaiming the Gay & Lesbian Past*, edited by Martin Duberman. This book has sections on the ancient world, pre-industrial societies, the nineteenth century, early twentieth century, and World War II and the postwar era. The book *Gay American History* by Jonathan Katz documents historical information on lesbians and gay men in the United States and has extensive bibliographies.

The video "Out of the Past" (see Appendix 11) is well worth showing in history classes. The award winning video traces the emergence of gay men and lesbians in American history through the eyes of a young woman coming to terms with herself. Its awards include the Sundance Film Festival Audience Award for Best Documentary in 1998.

Appendix 12 contains additional book titles that might be useful. If you have other book or video suggestions or comments please send them to Bob Latham, P.O. Box 70554, Point Richmond, CA 94807 or by E-mail to BobLatham@aol.com.

LIBRARIES

It is extremely important that school libraries include fiction with lesbian and gay characters as well as nonfiction that provide accurate information on all aspects of homosexuality.

Appendix 12 is a list of recommended books. A web search may be worth doing for newer titles. An easy method is to search topics on www.amazon.com. Also the GLSEN (Gay, Lesbian, Straight Education Network) website, www.glsen.org includes a useful resource titled BookLink. The free monthly GLBT literary e-zine posted on www.Q-zine.com frequently includes book reviews.

The Contra Costa Chapter of BANGLE (Bay Area Network of Gay and Lesbian Educators) donated books (15 different titles) to each high school in the county during 1992-93. They were carefully screened to be minimally controversial. In the West Contra Costa Unified School District, the books were reviewed by librarians and approved for inclusion in high school libraries by Associate Superintendent Anna Blackman. The BANGLE books are included in Appendix 12 and marked with an asterisk.

ELEMENTARY SCHOOLS

Elementary school teachers have a crucial opportunity to increase diversity tolerance. Most of the values and prejudices that students have at the secondary level are formed during their elementary school years. The following is recommended for elementary schools:

1. Name calling should not be allowed in the classroom or play yard. Slurs based on sexual orientation should be treated the same as slurs based on race, etc. (See Appendix 2.)

2. When referring to family units, recognition should be given to the fact that many families may include only one parent or other adult and some families may include two mothers or two fathers.

3. Stereotypes in sex roles -- what boys or girls choose in terms of toys, games, occupations, etc. -- should be avoided.

4. The use of non-judgmental language and a non-judgmental attitude toward sexual orientation and sex roles should be maintained.

There is now an excellent video resource available: "It's Elementary." All elementary school teachers and administrators should see it. The award winning video shows age appropriate lessons being taught in eight school districts across the country in grades kindergarten through eighth grade. It also shows why it is essential that information on sexual orientation be included at the elementary level. Two versions are available. The original 78-minute version is best for teachers who want to learn how to actually do the lessons. However there is a 37-minute excerpted version that may fit more easily into faculty meetings.

See Appendix 8 for a Workshop Design based on "It's Elementary."

"It's Elementary" was produced by Academy Award-Winner Debra Chasnoff and Helen Cohen of Women's Educational Media in San Francisco. Their more recent videos are also outstanding. "That's a Family" is perfect for showing to elementary students and covers several areas of discrimination. "Let's Get Real" covers name-calling and bullying and is great for 6 th grade and up. For full descriptions and video ordering information visit www.womedia.org or call 1-800-343.5540.

Another worthwhile video is "Both My Moms' Names Are Judy." It is a powerful 10-minute video that shows elementary school children who have gay or lesbian parents talking about their experiences at school. The video is available from Lesbian & Gay Parents Association, 260, Tingley Street, San Francisco, CA 94112, Phone: 415-337-1629, e-mail: LGPASF@aol.com.

Some books recommended for elementary classrooms are *Heather Has Two Mommies* by Leslea Newman, *Daddy's Roommate* by Michael Willhoite. *Asha's Mums* by Rosamund Elwin and Michele Paulse, *Is Your Family Like Mine* by Lois Abramchik, and *Molly's Family* by Nancy Garden. These books have been widely used and well received in many elementary classrooms. To be a bit more abstract, the Scholastic book *The Crayon Box That Talked* can be used to teach the meaning of diversity. See Appendix 12, page 67 for additional titles.

SITE AND DISTRICT ADMINISTRATION

There is a real need to increase the level of diversity tolerance towards sexual minorities in almost all school districts. The following steps are recommended:

1. *All* district personnel should attend at least one half-day workshop designed to reduce homophobia and heterosexism.

2. Accurate information on homosexuality should be included in all classes that teach sexuality.

3. Whenever diversity tolerance issues are raised, homophobia and heterosexism should be included.

4. Each high school should have at least one male and one female who receive additional training and are designated as "gay sensitive." They would cosponsor a student group such as a Gay-Straight Alliance when and if interest develops.

In Appendix 9 some recent court rulings that pertain to sexual orientation harassment are summarized. For example in 1996, there was a $900,000 out-of-court settlement after a jury ruled against middle and high school administrators who "violated a gay student's rights by not protecting him from years of harassment by other students." The material might be useful to provide a "bottom line" reason to prevent sexual orientation harassment.

EDUCATIONAL RESOURCES

(Includes National & San Francisco Bay Area)

Gay-Straight Alliance Network
160 14th Street
San Francisco, CA 94103
Phone: 415-552-4229 Website: www.gsanetwork.org
The website includes information about how to start a GSA, lists of hundreds of existing school GSAs, and an excellent monthly newsletter.

GLSEN (Gay, Lesbian and Straight Education Network)
121 West 27th Street, Suite 804
New York, NY 10001
Phone: 212-727-0135   E-mail: glsen@glsen.org Website: www.glsen.org
There are over 80 chapters nationwide.

GLSEN San Francisco-East Bay Chapter
1924 Grant St., Ste.4
Concord, CA 94520-2426
Phone: 925-685-5480 Website: www.glsen-sfeb.org

Pacific Center for Human Growth
2712 Telegraph Avenue   **Speakers Bureau**--A panel of three
Berkeley, CA 94705   speakers is usually provided. Excellent
Phone: 510-548-8283   for both classrooms and staff development.
Website: www.pacificcenter.org

PFLAG (Parents, Families and Friends of Lesbians and Gays)
1101 14th Street, N.W., Suite 1030
Washington, D.C. 20005
Phone: 202-638-4200 E-mail: info@pflag.org Website: www.pflag.org
Chapters nationwide provide excellent information and support for parents and children either together or separately.

PFLAG Fremont/East Bay Chapter
Phone: 510-226-6816

PFLAG San Francisco Chapter
Phone: 415-921-8850 E-mail: pflagsf@aol.com

YOUTH RESOURCES

AIDS Hot line   1-800-FOR-AIDS
(3 languages, all sexual orientations)

Gay-Straight Alliance Network
The website www.gsanetwork.org includes information about how to start a GSA, lists of hundreds of existing school GSAs, and an excellent monthly newsletter. Office: 160 14th Street, San Francisco, CA 94103, phone: 415-552-4229.

GLSEN (Gay, Lesbian, Straight Education Network)
National GLSEN's website, www.glsen.org has lots of information and many useful links.

LYRIC (Lavender Youth Recreation and Information Center)
Youth recording or talk line : 415-863-3636 and 1-800-246-PRIDE
Office: 415-703-6150, San Francisco, CA

The Trevor Project   1-800-850-8078
24-hour toll-free suicide hotline for gay and questioning youth. Teens can talk to trained counselors, find local resources and take important steps on their way to becoming healthy adults. All calls are free and confidential.
Website: www.trevorproject.com

Pacific Center for Human Growth
2712 Telegraph Avenue, Berkeley, CA 94705
Phone: 510-548-8283 Website: www.pacificcenter.org
Information, support groups (including for men and women under 23), clinical services, HIV/AIDS counseling, speakers bureau, etc.

PFLAG (Parents & Friends of Lesbians and Gays)
Excellent information and Support Groups. Youth may attend alone or with parents.. Some local chapters in San Francisco Bay Area, CA:
Berkeley: 510-562-7692 Fremont: 510-226-6816 Oakland: 510-562-7692
San Francisco: 415-921-8850 and pflagsf@aol.com Walnut Creek: 925-282-8928

Rainbow Community Center
Includes Support Groups for Youth
2637 Pleasant Hill Road, Pleasant Hill, CA 94523
Phone: 925-210-0563 Website: www.rainbowcc.org

APPENDIX 1:
HOMOSEXUALITY AND THE BIBLE:
WHAT YOU REALLY NEED TO KNOW

Sodomy: The word sodomy comes from the story of Sodom and Gomorrah (Genesis 19). The sin described was homosexual rape by heterosexual men intent on humiliating their visitors by treating them like women.

Other Ambiguous References to Homosexuality: The language in 1 Corinthians 6:9 and 1 Timothy 1:10 is unclear whether the problematic issue is homosexuality or the promiscuity and prostitution the Hebrew authors automatically associated with homosexual behavior. Compare this to the media portrayals of homosexuality in the 1970's which focused on the gay bar scenes in San Francisco and New York City.

The Passages Most Commonly Used to Condemn Homosexuality

Leviticus 18:22: You shall not lie with a male as with a woman; it is an abomination.

Leviticus 20:13: If a man lies with a male as with a woman, both of them have committed an abomination; they shall be put to death; their blood is upon them.

These passages are based on patriarchal, pre-scientific Hebrew assumptions. When a male acted like a female, it was considered a degradation of male dignity. Since semen was thought to be the sole source of life, its spilling for any reason other than procreation was considered an abomination (this included masturbation as well as homosexual acts). This was an understandable value in a growing, tribal society. For further emphasis, note that for women, masturbation and homosexual acts were never forbidden nor discussed in the Bible.

Romans 1:26-27: For this reason, God gave them up to dishonorable passions. Their women exchanged natural relations for unnatural, and the men likewise gave up natural relations with women and were consumed with passion for one another, men committing shameful acts with men and receiving in their own persons the due penalty for their error.

Paul assumes that homosexuality is contrary to nature, when in fact, extensive research shows that it is not. Thus Paul was wrong to condemn homosexuals for deviating from a "natural heterosexual state."

Sex Before Marriage: The church has long forbidden sex outside the context of marriage. On this basis people condemn homosexuals for having premarital sexual relations, even though the church denies them the right to marry. However the Bible nowhere explicitly prohibits sexual relations between unmarried consenting adults. Song of Songs even describes a love affair between an unmarried couple.

Do We Interpret the Bible? The Bible permits slavery, prostitution, polygamy and having concubines, which modern American culture overwhelmingly rejects. Meanwhile, the Bible forbids divorce, remarriage, nudity (even in front of your spouse), intercourse during menstruation, and perpetuates the assumptions that women are the sexual property of men and that semen and menstrual blood are unclean. Clearly, we as Christians choose what we do and do not follow in scripture by weighing relevancy and popular opinion.

What Would Jesus Do? Jesus never says anything about the issue of homosexuality. However, in Luke 12:57 Jesus says "Why do you not judge for yourselves what is right?" Just as we did for the abolitionist movement and the women's movement, we must throw aside the cultural assumptions of the Bible and follow the primary commandment Jesus gave us of loving our neighbor as ourselves and loving God with all our heart.

For Further Reading:

"Biblical Perspectives on Homosexuality," *The Christian Century*, Nov. 7, 1979.
Claiming the Promise: An Ecumenical Welcoming Bible Study Resource on Homosexuality, Reconciling Congregation Program, 3801 N. Keeler Ave., Chicago IL 60641
What the Bible Really Says About Homosexuality by Daniel Helminiak
Rescuing the Bible from Fundamentalism by John Shelby Spong
Homosexuality in the Church: Both Sides of the Debate by Jeffrey S. Siker
Is the Homosexual My Neighbor? by Letha Dawson Scanzoni and Virginia Ramey Mollenkott
Christianity, Social Tolerance, and Homosexuality by John Boswell
Gay Theology Without Apology by Gary David Comstock
New Testament and Homosexuality by Robin Scroggs
Dirt, Greed and Sex by William Countrymen

For More Information on Religion and GLBT Concerns

Affirmation: United Methodist for Lesbian, Gay and Bisexual Concerns
    P.O. Box 1021
    Evanston, IL 60204

Association of Welcoming & Affirming Baptists (American Baptist)
    P.O. Box 2596
    Attleboro Falls, MA 02763
    Phone/Fax: 508-226-1945

Dignity/USA (Roman Catholic)
    1500 Massachusetts Ave NW, Ste. 11
    Washington DC 20005
    Phone: 202-861-0017; 800-877-8797
    Fax: 202-429-9808
    E-mail: dignity@aol.com

Gay, Lesbian and Affirming Disciples Alliance (Disciples of Christ)
    P.O. Box 19223
    Indianapolis, IN 46219-0223
    Phone: 212-288-3246
    Fax: 212-288-7602

Integrity, Inc. (Episcopal)
    P.O. Box 5255
    New York, NY 10185-5255
    Phone: 908-220-1914

Metropolitan Community Church (MCC)
    8704 Santa Monica Blvd., 2nd Floor
    West Hollywood, CA 90069-4548
    Phone: 310-360-8640
    Fax: 310-360-8680
    Website: www. ufmcc.com

More Light Churches Network (Presbyterian USA)
    5525 Timber Lane
    Excelsior, MN 55331
    Phone: 612-470-0093

The Oasis (Episcopal)
 31 Mulberry Street
 Newark, NJ 07102
 Phone: 201-621-8151
 Fax: 201-622-3503
 e-mail: theoasisnj@aol.com

Open and Affirming Program of the United Church Coalition for Lesbian/Gay Concerns (United Church of Christ)
 P.O. Box 403
 Holden, MA 01520-0403
 Phone: 508-856-9316
 Fax: 508-852-3559

Reconciled in Christ Program of Lutherans Concerned/North America (Lutheran)
 2466 Sharondale Drive
 Atlanta, GA 30305
 Phone/Fax: 404-266-9615

Reconciling Congregation Program (United Methodist)
 3801 North Keeler Ave
 Chicago, IL 60641
 Phone: 773-736-5526
 Fax: 773-736-5475

Supportive Congregations Network of the Brethren/Mennonite Council for Lesbian and Gay Concerns
 P.O. Box 6300
 Minneapolis, MN 55406
 Phone: 612-305-0315
 E-mail: SCNetwork@aol.com

APPENDIX 2:
SLURS

Name-Calling

Name-calling involving sexual orientation is extremely harmful and common. As reported in The Des Moines Register (March 7, 1997), the typical high school student hears anti-gay slurs 25.5 times a day. Basically, sexual orientation slurs should be treated exactly the same as racial slurs. Neither should be tolerated.

Anti-slur policies may and should be adopted at the district level. For example, the San Francisco Board of Education has Board Policy 5162, which views the use of "slurs against any person on the basis of race, color, creed, national origin, ancestry, age, sex, sexual orientation, or disability" as unacceptable behavior. Their *SFUSD Student Handbook* prescribes clear disciplinary guidelines to be implemented when slurs do occur.

Alta Loma High School has a similar policy:

"All students at Alta Loma are expected to respect others in word, deed and action. We do not tolerate language that insults any person on the basis of race, religion, gender, sexual orientation, disability or appearance."

The consequences for anti-slur violations at Alta Loma High School may be worth emulating. If a student violates the policy, that student is sent to the office and given a series of questions to answer. The questions are copied on the next page. Amy Goldman, a teacher at the school, says the policy "has really improved our school climate."

The following are a series of questions which you are expected to answer with honesty and sincerity. These need to be turned in to the Vice Principal immediately after you have completed them.

1. What did you say that brought you to the office today?

2. Why did you say it? What did you hope to accomplish by saying this?

3. What does this statement mean or imply?

4. Why is what you said hurtful? It is not acceptable to say "I didn't mean anything by it."

5. How would you feel if someone made a comment that insulted you based on your race, religion, gender, sexual orientation, disability, or appearance?

6. How do you think others felt when you made this comment?

7. How does it hurt our school when students put each other down?

8. What will you do differently in the future to make sure you don't hurt people?

On a separate sheet of paper, write a letter to your parent/guardian explaining why you have spent this period in the attendance office instead of in your regular learning environment. This letter needs to be signed by your parent/ guardian, initialed by an administrator and returned to the teacher before you will be admitted back to class.

Irrespective of district policy, each classroom teacher can and should enforce a slur-free environment within their classroom. The following exercise may be helpful to accomplish that goal:

1. Have students brainstorm names they have heard someone called.
2. List all suggestions on the board.
3. Discuss the following categories, and group names accordingly:
   racial   sexual   ethnic   sexual orientation   religious
   size   ability   gender   etc.
4. Educate students that all name-calling involves prejudice and is harmful.
5. State that none of the listed names is acceptable in your classroom and that name-calling will not be tolerated.
6. Explain why and discuss possible consequences.
7. Discuss how students can become allies of victims of name-calling.

Amy Goldman suggest this **Lesson on Slurs**:

Objective: Students will develop empathy for others, through personal identification, and realize how devastating words can be when they are used as weapons. This is part of the education component of our Anti-Slur Policy.

Activity I: Brainstorm (10 to 15 minutes)
Students will generate a list of categories covering all of the aspects of a person's identity and appearance. For example, race, gender, sexual orientation, disabilities, religion etc. might be included.

Then students give examples of specific put-downs and list those under the correct category. For instance "four eyes" would go under the disability column.

Activity II: Reflective Writing Assignment 3 choices (10 minutes)
a. Students will write about a time when they were personally put down or slurred. Explain what happened, how they responded, and what they felt.
b. Students write about a time when they harassed another person for one or more of the above reasons. Explain what happened, why they did it, and how they felt.
c. (If they can't do a or b) Students write about a time when they witnessed someone else being put down and say what they saw, how they responded, what they wish they could have done/will do next time, and how they felt.

Optional: Whole Class or Small Group Discussion (varies)
You may want to give students a chance to read their incidence out loud as part of an extended discussion. Also the group can decide some appropriate ways to respond to slurs in the future if they occur.

Activity III: Group Anti-Slur Poster Project (20 minutes or more)
In small groups students will design a poster showing that slurs are a form of violence that must be stopped.

Jokes

Jokes can be just as harmful as name-calling. Jokes about homosexuals or any of the other targeted groups can and should be discouraged by saying, for example:

> "That sort of joke is offensive and will not be tolerated in this classroom." or
> "Jokes about any religious, racial, or sexual group are unacceptable in this classroom." or
> "Jokes that make fun of people are unacceptable in this classroom."

Teasing

Cathy Figel's response to the question: "How do I handle two middle school girls being teased and called lesbians?":

I have a couple of thoughts on your situation: My first is the issue is not about the girls being lesbian or not, it is about being harassed.

My next thought is that if your staff is as educated and supportive as you report then this issue should be brought to the forefront by the entire staff. If everyone knows that these two girls are being taunted, then it should be addressed by everyone in front of everyone. What I would suggest is each teacher addressing it during advisory/homeroom. If the students hear all the teachers acknowledge what is going on and that this type of teasing is not allowed at your school it will make it very clear as to what is acceptable.

After the Colorado killings I talked to all my classes (grades 6-8 physical education) about the impact of teasing and out-casting classmates. I also went over that I can't be everywhere and hear everything so they have a responsibility to speak up. We practiced saying two things: "Stop that it is not nice" to the student doing the teasing and "Are you OK?" to the student being teased. I have since continued to remind them of their responsibility and when I hear teasing or it is reported to me, I go back to the group and ask them what they should have said. We have to make sure that we give the children the skills and empower them to take action.

And specifically for the girls . . . I would have a meeting with students who you can identify as previously being their friends or students who are strong/sensitive leaders (maybe about 20) and talk to them about the situation, personalize it for them, and ask for their support on helping these girls feel happy at school. Again this would need daily inquiries of asking this group individually how the girls are feeling . . .reminding them of your expectation to support the girls.

Lastly I would also make sure that the girls' parents are aware of the teasing and the need for support at home.

APPENDIX 3:
FACTS & STATISTICS

Just the Facts... On GLBT Students and Schools
From The P.E.R.S.O.N. Project (Public Education Regarding Sexual Orientation Nationally), Jean Richter -- richter@eecs.berkeley.edu.

1. Self-Realization

Gay male adolescents report becoming aware of a distinct feeling of "being different" between ages 5-7; they also report that they did not yet connect this feeling to the issue of sexuality. [1]

The median age at which lesbian and gay youth become aware that their feelings of "difference" are linked to a same-sex sexual orientation is 13. [2]

9% of high school students identify as "gay, lesbian, bisexual or questioning." [3]

2. The School Climate--Student Attitudes

"We were picked on. We were called 'queer' and 'faggot' and a host of other homophobic slurs. We were also used as punching bags by our classmates, just for being different." -- college student, remembering high school*

97% of students in public high schools report regularly hearing homophobic remarks from their peers. [4]

The typical high school student hears anti-gay slurs 25.5 times a day. [5]

80% of gay and lesbian youth report severe social isolation. [6]

Staff Attitudes

"I realize that children can be very cruel, but when teachers and adults encourage or do not discourage mean and cruel behavior it makes me angry and very sad." -- a parent of a gay child

53% of students report hearing homophobic comments made by school staff. [7]

80% of prospective teachers report negative attitudes toward gay and lesbian people. [8]

1/3 of prospective teachers can be classified as "high-grade homophobes." [9]

52% of prospective teachers report that they would feel uncomfortable working with an openly lesbian or gay colleague. [10]

77% of prospective teachers would not encourage a class discussion on homosexuality; 85% oppose integrating gay/lesbian themes into their existing curricula. [11]

Two-thirds of guidance counselors harbor negative feelings toward gay and lesbian people. [12]

Less than 20% of guidance counselors have received any training on serving gay and lesbian students. [13]

Only 25% of guidance counselors consider themselves "highly competent" in serving gay and lesbian youth. [14]

Teachers fail to intervene in 97% of incidents involving anti-gay slurs at school. [15]

78% of school administrators say they know of no lesbian, gay, or bisexual students in their schools, yet 94% of them claim they feel their schools are safe places for these young people. [16]

3. The Family

"On reflecting about homosexuality, I've learned that: my religious tradition taught me to believe that my son was a sinner; my medical support system taught me to believe that my son was sick; my educational system taught me that my son was abnormal; my legal system views my son and his partner in an unsanctioned relationship without legal rights and protection that are afforded my married daughter; my family, immediate and extended, provided no acknowledgment or support for having a gay relative in its midst; my major communications sources treated homosexuality as deviant." -- father of a gay son

28% of American households consist of married parents with biological children; 7% consist of married parents with children where a father who works outside the home and the mother at home. [17]

19% of gay men and 25% of lesbians report suffering physical violence at the hands of family members as a result of their sexual orientation. [18]

11.5 % of gay and lesbian youth report being physically attacked by family members. [19]

26% of adolescent gay males report having to leave home as a result of conflicts with their family over their sexual orientation. [20]

42% of homeless youth self-identify as gay/lesbian. [21]

4. Anti-Gay Violence and Harassment

"I just began hating myself more and more, as each year the hatred towards me grew and escalated from just simple name-calling in elementary school to having persons in high school threaten to beat me up, being pushed and dragged around the ground, having hands slammed in lockers, and a number of other daily tortures." -- a gay male high school student

"Homosexuals are probably the most frequent victims [of hate crimes]" in the U.S. [22]

45% of gay males and 20% of lesbians report having experienced verbal harassment and/or physical violence as a result of their sexual orientation during high school. [23]

19% of gay/lesbian youth report suffering physical attacks based on their sexual orientation. [24]

15% of LGB youth have been injured so badly in a physical attack at school that they have had to seek the services of a doctor or nurse. [25]

20% of LGB youth report skipping school at least once a month because of feeling unsafe while there. [22]

42% of adolescent lesbians and 34% of adolescent gay males who have suffered physical attack also attempt suicide. [21]

5. Health Issues

"Due to societal fear and ignorance, my teachers and counselors labeled my confusion as rebellion, and placed me in the category of a troubled discipline problem. But still I had nothing to identify with and no role models to guide me, to help me sort out this confusion, and I began to believe that I was simply alone. A few weeks into my sophomore year, I woke up in a psych hospital after taking my father's camping knife violently to my wrists and hoping for success." -- lesbian student

1 in 5 HIV-positive men were apparently infected during their adolescent years. [28]

68% of adolescent gay males use alcohol (26% or more at least once a week); 44% use other drugs. [29]

83% of adolescent lesbians use alcohol and 56% use other drugs. [30]

31% of LGB students have used cocaine as opposed to 7% of non-LGB students. [31]

62% of LGB students smoke as opposed to 35% of non-LGB students. [32]

32% of LGB students has gotten pregnant or gotten someone pregnant as opposed to 12% of non-LGB students. [33]

30% of gay and bisexual adolescent males attempt suicide at least once. [34]

Gay and lesbian youth represent 30% of all completed teen suicide: extrapolation shows this means a successful suicide attempt by a gay teen every 5 hours and 48 minutes. [35]

LGB students are four times more likely to attempt suicide than non-LGB students. [36]

End Notes

* Testimonies are from the public hearings conducted by the Massachusetts Governor's Commission on Gay and Lesbian Youth, 1992. Governor William Weld, R-MA.

1 Treadway, Leo, and Yoakum, John. "Creating a Safer School Environment for Lesbian and Gay Student," in Journal of School Health, September, 1992.

2 Sears, James. *Growing Up Gay in the South*. New York: Harrington Park Press, 1991.

3 Seattle Public Schools, "1995 Seattle Teen Health Risk Survey," reprinted in Third Annual Report of the Safe Schools Anti-Violence Documentation Project, 1996.

4 "Making Schools Safe for Gay and Lesbian Youth: Report of the Massachusetts Governor's Commission on Gay and Lesbian Youth," 1993.

5 Carter, Kellye, "Gay Slurs Abound," in The Des Moines Register, March 7, 1997, p. 1.

6 Hetrick, Emery, and Martin, A. Damien. "Developmental Issues and Their Resolution for Gay and Lesbian Adolescents, " in Journal of Homosexuality, 1987.

7 "Making Schools Safe for Gay and Lesbian Youth: Report of the Massachusetts Governor's Commission on Gay and Lesbian Youth," 1993.

8 Sears, James. "Educators, Homosexuality, and Homosexual Students: Are Personal Feelings Related to Professional Beliefs?" in Harbeck, Karen, ed. *Coming Out of the Classroom Closet*. New York: Harrington Park Press, 1992.

9 ibid.

10 ibid.

11 ibid.

12 ibid.

13 ibid.

14 Price, James H., and Telljohan, Susan. "School Counselors' Perceptions of Adolescent Homosexuals" in Journal of School Health, Dec. 1991.

15 Carter, Kellye, "Gay Slurs Abound," in The Des Moines Register, March 7, 1997, p. 1.

16 GLSEN/Detroit, "Bruised Bodies, Bruised Spirits: An Assessment of the Current Climate of Safety for Gay, Lesbian, and Bisexual Youth in Southeastern Michigan Schools," pp. 31-33.

17 1990 U.S. Census Report.

18 Philadelphia Lesbian and Gay Task Force, "Discrimination and Violence toward Lesbian Women and Gay Men in Philadelphia and the Commonwealth of Pennsylvania," 1992.

19 Hetrick-Martin Institute "Violence Report," 1988.

20 Remafedi, Gary. "Male Homosexuality: The Adolescent's Perspective," in Pediatrics, 1987.

21 Victim Services/Traveler's Aid, "Streetwork Project Study," 1991.

22 U.S. Department of Justice, "The Response of the Criminal Justice System to Bias Crime: An Exploratory View," 1987.

23 National Gay and Lesbian Task Force, "National Anti-Gay/Lesbian Victimization Report," 1984.

24 Hetrick-Martin Institute "Violence Report," 1988.

25 Seattle Public Schools, "1995 Seattle Teen Health Risk Survey," reprinted in Third Annual Report of the Safe Schools Anti-Violence Documentation Project, 1996.

26 The Centers for Disease Control and the Massachusetts Department of Education, "The Massachusetts Youth Risk Behavior Survey," 1995.

27 Hetrick-Martin Institute "Violence Report," 1988.

28 Centers for Disease Control figures, 1995.

29 Hunter, Joyce, et al. unpublished research by the Columbia University HIV Center for Clinical and Behavior Studies, 1992.

30 ibid.

31 The Centers for Disease Control and the Massachusetts Department of Education, "The Massachusetts Youth Risk Behavior Survey," 1995.

32 ibid.

33 ibid.

34 Remafedi, Gary, et al. "Risk Factors for Attempted Suicide in Gay and Bisexual Youth," in Pediatrics (1991).

35 Gibson, Paul. "U.S. Department of Health and Human Services Secretary's Task Force on Youth Suicide Report," 1989. See also Remafedi, Gary. "Death by Denial: Studies of Gay and Lesbian Youth Suicide" (Boston: Alyson Publications, 1995).

36 The Centers for Disease Control and the Massachusetts Department of Education, "The Massachusetts Youth Risk Behavior Survey," 1995.

===

Jean Richter -- richter@eecs.berkeley.edu
The P.E.R.S.O.N. Project (Public Education Regarding Sexual Orientation Nationally)
CHECK OUT OUR INFO-LOADED WEB PAGE AT:
http://www.youth.org/loco/PERSONProject/

APPENDIX 4:
DISCUSSION POINTS FOR "A QUIZ ON GAY AND LESBIAN ISSUES"

Having collected the Quiz, state that all of the statements are false but are based on common stereotypes that many people incorrectly believe to be true. Spend time as needed to convince the group that the statements are, in fact, false. Below are some hints on how to do that.

1. "Lesbian/gay people can ordinarily be identified by certain mannerisms or physical characteristics" is false. Although some people are easily identified, most are not. After learning that a group of medical professionals were unconvinced by my assertions and anecdotes, I wrote the essay "Can You Spot an UP?" on the next page. I would suggest copying it for use only if you think it is important to change a group's belief. For example, I might use it for a group of medical professionals but probably not for a high school biology class.

2. "Homosexual behavior is found only in humans (not animals)" is false. Scientists have observed homosexual activity throughout the animal world. According to the book *Biological Exuberance: Animal Homosexuality and Natural Diversity* by Bruce Bagemihl (751 pages, St. Martin's Press, 1999), biologists over two centuries have observed bi, trans and gay activities in at least 450 species--including reptiles, fish and insects. Males caress and kiss, showing tenderness instead of aggression. Females form long-lasting bonds or may meet for sexual encounters as passionate as they are brief. Animals of the same sex build nests and homes; many pairs raise young without members of the opposite sex in attendance. Others have partners of both sexes, or live in communal groups in which everybody has sex with everybody else. Estimates are that same-sex relationships probably occur in from 15 to 30 percent of the 1 million species that are known to exist.

3. "We know what causes homosexuality" remains false. Recent research indicates that people's sexual orientation is probably already determined at birth, but that has not yet been proven. However, expert testimony in court has established that sexual orientation is determined before school age. Learning the facts about sexual orientation will not cause anyone to develop an orientation that does not already exist.

Can You Spot an UP?

An UP, or Underwear Purple person has a compulsion to wear purple underwear, to have purple cloth next to his or her skin. Most only wear purple underwear (either boxer or bikini.) A few, however, also wear purple shirts or blouses and sometimes purple socks. They are obvious to everyone.

This may be easier to follow if we think of a village of 100 people. In this typical village, 90 people wear white underwear and 10 people wear purple underwear. Of the 10 people who wear purple underwear, one also wears purple shirts and purple socks.

Everyone can see the purple shirt. Everyone knows that he is an UP. The UPs who do not wear purple shirts or blouses or socks (but who always wear purple underwear) remain unrecognized, invisible. Even though these UPs have frequent contact with everyone in the village, no one knows that they are UPs because their purple underwear is covered.

Most people in the village say "Yes, I can recognize an UP," and they think of the one who always wears purple shirts. They do not realize that they pass 9 other UPs every day without recognizing them. Thus UPs are an "invisible minority" in the village.

- - - - - - - - - - - - - - - - - - - -

I wrote the story above because it is often difficult for people to accept the fact that they cannot **usually** identify sexual orientation by appearance. I have been a member of many gay organization where there were few or no "purple shirts." These organizations have included running clubs, scuba clubs, book clubs, and environmental clubs as well as college alumni and education groups. I have also been a member of similar non-gay organizations. The members of the gay and the members of the non-gay organizations **look and act the same**.

Lack of visibility is important because it contributes to heterosexism, the assumption that everyone is heterosexual. Heterosexism is pervasive in our society and destructive to people who are or will eventually identify themselves as gay, lesbian, bisexual, or transgender.

4. "Most lesbian/gay people can be cured by having really good sex with a member of the opposite sex" is false. In fact, many lesbian and gay people do have sex with members of the opposite sex before realizing and accepting their homosexuality. Similarly, many heterosexual adults have had one or more homosexual experiences.

5. "The majority of child molesters are lesbian/gay" is false. It is important to deal with this statement forcefully and effectively. Whether or not it is articulated, this incorrect stereotype is a major contributor to homophobia.

In a presentation I usually hold up a copy of a booklet from the local police department (*Missing Juveniles, Sexual Assault & Child Abuse Prevention Manual*, Richmond Police Officers Association) and read from it:

"From 'A Study of the Child Molester: Myths and Realities' we learn that the heterosexual adult constitutes a higher risk of sexual victimization to the underage child than does the homosexual adult.... Offenders attracted to boy victims typically report that they are uninterested in or repulsed by adult homosexual relationships.... A large majority (83%) of these subjects led exclusively heterosexual adult lives, and the remaining (17%) were bisexually orientated."

6. "Lesbian/gay people should not be teachers or parents because they will try to convert young people into the gay lifestyle" is false. Lesbian and gay people want their students or children to have whatever sexual orientation is natural for that student or child. Most lesbian and gay people were raised by heterosexual parents. Most children raised by lesbian and gay people turn out to be heterosexual.

7. "Lesbian/gay people have made a conscious decision to be that way" is false. The video "Gay Youth" will show how false the statement is. Most lesbian and gay people go through a period of trying to deny their sexual orientation due to the lack of support and discrimination that exists in our society.

8. "Gay/lesbian parents raise gay/lesbian children" is false. See 6 above. About 10% of the children of gay/lesbian parents are gay or lesbian, the same percentage as for straight parents.

9. "Homosexuality is a type of mental illness and can be cured by appropriate psychotherapy" is false. Both the American Psychiatric and the American Psychological Associations have rejected any connection between homosexuality and mental illness.

10. "One homosexual experience as an adolescent will play a large part in determining whether a person will be homosexually oriented as an adult" is false. According to the Kinsey report, a significant percent of the adult heterosexual population has had at least one same-sex experience at some point in their life, generally during early adolescence.

Additional points that may be worth making:

1. People who are secure and comfortable with their own sexuality usually do not have a problem being around GLBT people.

2. Research by US psychologist Prof. Adams of the University of Georgia suggests that 80 percent of men who are homophobic have secret homosexual feelings. In Prof. Adams's test, homophobic men who said they were exclusively heterosexual were shown gay sex videos. Four out of five became sexually aroused by the homoerotic imagery. (Prof. Adams's research was published in the prestigious US Journal of Abnormal Psychology in 1996, with the backing of the American Psychological Association.)

These findings support the theories that homophobia (fear and hatred of gayness and support for antigay discrimination) is often indicative of repressed, self-loathing homosexual feelings; and that some homophobes subconsciously use antigay attitudes as a smokescreen to disguise their own homosexuality.

APPENDIX 5: BISEXUALITY

The Kinsey Scale

Dr. Alfred Kinsey and his associates in the late 1940s and early 1950s pioneered extensive research on sexuality. His results have been supported by more recent research by Masters and Johnson and by others.

One of the most important results from the studies is that there is a broad spectrum of sexual orientation, not just two lifestyles. Kinsey developed a seven-point continuum based on the degree of sexual responsiveness people have to the members of the same and other sex:

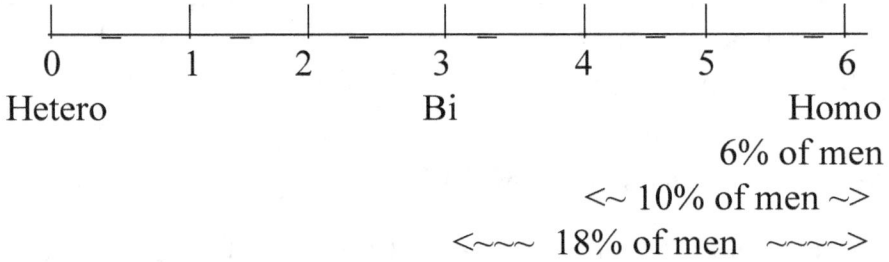

0 = Exclusively heterosexual
1 = Predominantly heterosexual, incidentally homosexual
2 = Predominantly heterosexual, but more than incidentally homosexual
3 = Equally heterosexual and homosexual
4 = Predominantly homosexual, but more than incidentally heterosexual
5 = Predominantly homosexual, incidentally heterosexual
6 = Exclusively homosexual

Kinsey used a variety of activities in assessing an individual's ranking on the continuum including:
Fantasies
Dreams
Thoughts
Frequency of sexual activity
Emotional feelings
Note that sexual activity is only one of several indicators.

Some Famous Bisexuals (?)

SHAKESPEARE (New York Daily News, February 26, 1999)
"Shakespeare in Love" director John Madden claims as convincing as Paltrow and Fiennes are as lovers in the movie, Madden is the first to admit the Bard of Avon might actually have been gay.

"At the very least, he was bisexual," Madden tells us. "The first group of his sonnets were dedicated to a man with the initials WH."

The director notes that his movie alludes to the "sexual ambiguity" of the Elizabethan stage, where "boy actors dressed as girls who sometimes pretended to be boys."

"I wouldn't make claims in any direction, except to say that Shakespeare is probably more than anything we imagine him to be," he said. "I should guess he was pan-sexual. It's impossible for me to believe he could write about love and sexual passion without having experienced it firsthand."

PRESIDENT LINCOLN
Larry Kramer, the Oscar-nominated screenwriter and founder of ACT-UP, told a group of activists that the 16th president of the United States, Abraham Lincoln, was gay.

Kramer told the audience that a 28-year-old Lincoln carried on a four-year affair with a 24 year-old shop owner, Joshua Speed.

"Between 1839 and 1842 Abraham Lincoln and Joshua Speed loved each other," Kramer said definitively. After 1842, they loved each other but not as strongly, Kramer said. Both eventually married, as dictated by the standards of the age, but neither coupling was happy.

Kramer says Lincoln met Speed shortly after his arrival in Springfield, Illinois in 1839. Speed offered the gangly and overly tall Lincoln space in his bed above the store he ran. Lincoln accepted.

APPENDIX 6:
STUDENT SUPPORT GROUPS

Gay-Straight Alliances

Every high school should have some sort of peer support system for GLBT and questioning students. A student Gay-Straight Alliance (GSA) seems to be an effective organization to provide that support.

I started a GSA at my conservative suburban high school in 1994. Some students came for basic information. Many came because they had GLBT friends and/ or family members. Each meeting started by going around the circle, stating names, and giving each person the chance to speak about a relevant problem or event that occurred since the last meeting. We often had special presentations about topics of interest and we did projects to increase tolerance at the school. Obviously there are many possible formats and it is best to use input from the participants.

The Gay-Straight Alliance Network is an excellent, recently established, resource. Their website, **www.gsanetwork.org** provides useful information about how to start a GSA, lists hundreds of existing school GSAs and provides a monthly newsletter. Contact information:

> Gay-Straight Alliance Network
> 160 14th Street
> San Francisco, CA 94103
> Phone: 415-552-4229

GLSEN provides a national network of students working against homophobia in high schools, providing support, resources, and connections so that starting and sustaining Gay-Straight Alliances and similar groups will be easier. It is called Student Pride. The website is www.glsen.org/pages/sections/involved/ studentpride/.

Student Pride offers three e-mail listserves designed to network students activists from around the country:

• GSA TALK is a discussion list of high school GSA organizers from around the country. To subscribe send an e-mail to glsenlists@glsen.org with SUBSCRIBE GSATALK in the body of the message.

44

• ADVISOR TALK is a discussion list of the faculty/staff advisors of high school GSA organizers from around the country. To subscribe send an e-mail to glsenlists@glsen.org with SUBSCRIBE ADVISORTALK in the body of the message.

• STUDENT PRIDE ALERT is a READ-ONLY list of news and announcements from Student Pride. To subscribe send an e-mail to glsenlists@glsen.org with SUBSCRIBE STDNTPRIDEALERT in the body of the message.

Some Suggestions on Getting a GSA Started

Penny J. Culliton started a GSA in rural New Hampshire and offers some suggestions and insights that you may find useful: Below is information about Monadnock Outright, a gay/straight youth alliance in a rural area (NOT meeting in a school) for ages 14-22. I no longer am active in the group's board of directors (I'm a straight ally and always intended that the group should be run by sexual minorities anyway) but was its founder (that is, it was my brainchild, and I started it with the help of 2-3 other adults).

THIS IS HOW I GOT THE GROUP STARTED:

1. I asked at a local P-FLAG meeting who was interested.

2. I used lists I had gotten from attending various conferences; on these lists were people who had signed up as being interested in supporting l/g/b/t youth.

3. I sent forms out asking if the above people were still interested (with SASE).

4. I checked with a local youth center to see when time and space would be available and how much it would cost ($10) per session.

5. Another P-FLAGer (gay man, late forties) knew several wonderful people who were interested in helping form the group; we did not get any youth interest at first.

6. I took all the positive responses from interested adults and then sent each one of those people a form asking what night (Sunday and Thursday were the 2 possibilities) they could facilitate a two-hour meeting once or twice a month. I also set up an initial planning meeting at the youth center.

7. We all met that night for the planning session, called ourselves the Board of Directors, and ironed out the details.

8. I obtained copies of Seacoast Outright's guidelines and we used these plus our own experience in writing our own guidelines.

9. We ran ads (some paid and some PSAs) in the local papers, and I sent out mailings to the Health, English/Drama, and Guidance departments of all local high schools. We also announced in gay/lesbian newsletters.

10. I designed and printed up fliers and posters. A person on the Board with a copier made copies and we posted them in libraries and post offices as well as some restaurants, stores and health-clubs. When we saw someone had removed one, we put it back up.

11. WE WAITED A MONTH before any youths showed up. You have to be patient!! We now even have youth Board members.

HERE IS THE LETTER WE SEND OUT TO SCHOOLS AND CHURCHES, AS WELL AS COUNSELORS, ETC. :

Monadnock Outright's mission is to provide a safe, drug-free, and confidential way for gay, lesbian, bisexual, and questioning youths as well as their friends and allies to meet, share experiences, form friendships, and learn from one another. We have been going strong since February of 1995!

Meetings are held every Thursday from 7-8:30 PM at The Place to Go on Route 202 North in Peterborough (46 Concord Street, next to Monadnock Worksource).

Meetings are facilitated by adult volunteers, who are dedicated to ending the isolation and silence that are so often a problem for our gay youth and their friends. One of our main goals is to help curb the loss of self-esteem that all too often pushes our youth towards substance abuse and suicide. In addition to support and socializing, we provide a small library with books and magazines and plan to show educational videos as well as feature guest speakers when possible. Beyond that, Monadnock Outright's direction is determined by the youths who attend our meetings.

If you have any questions at all, please call Penny Culliton, at... ; or Gordon Sherman at.... Our mailing address is 2 Putnam St. #1, Wilton, NH 03086, in care of Penny Culliton.

THIS IS THE FORM USED WHEN AN ADULT WANTS TO VOLUNTEER AS A FACILITATOR:

Name:_____ Age:_____

Nick Name:_____ Date:_____

Check one: _____ Gay Man _____Lesbian _____Bisexual: ___M___F
               _____ Hetero. Ally: ___M ___F

Address:

_____

Home phone:_____ Best times to call:_____

Work phone: _____ Best times to call:_____

Occupation/Place of employment: _____

If you need additional space on any of the following questions, feel free to attach an additional page.

1. Why do you want to join MONADNOCK OUTRIGHT?

2. What perspectives to you bring to MONADNOCK OUTRIGHT? What message do you have to offer to the young people with whom you come in contact?

3. What experience have you had, if any, with youth groups, public speaking, leading workshops, counseling, helping, community outreach, fund raising, or publicity

4. How do you feel about being gay, lesbian, or bisexual (or if you're an ally, how do you feel about gay, lesbian, bisexual people)? What role does your

sexual orientation play in your life? Have you ever participated in gay, lesbian or bisexual groups, activities, or events? If so, which ones?

5. Please discuss your awareness of forms of oppression other than homophobia, including details of your own background and experience. What are the strong and weak points in your awareness? Have you been active in trying to end other forms of oppression? If so, how?

6. Is there anything else you would like us to know about you?

7. What personal experiences with gay, lesbian, and bisexual people and/or with homophobia have most influenced you?

8. Discuss the range of things a heterosexual person can do to be a good ally to bisexual, lesbian, and gay people. In what ways have you tried to be a good ally?

9. MONADNOCK OUTRIGHT is structured to allow maximum participation in decision making by all of its members by consensus, while still leaving final control to its Board. How do you feel about this organizational structure?

THESE ARE THE ADULT VOLUNTEER POLICIES AND GUIDELINES FOR OUR FACILITATORS:

THE VOLUNTEER IS IN A UNIQUE ROLE TO HAVE FIRST LINE CONTACT WITH YOUTH MEMBERS AND IDENTIFY THE VARIED NEEDS THAT MAY BE EXPRESSED BY THESE INDIVIDUALS. SPECIFICALLY, THE VOLUNTEER IS IN A POSITION TO USE THAT INFORMATION TO 1) GUIDE YOUTH TO APPROPRIATE RESOURCES, 2) ENCOURAGE IMPROVED SOCIAL INTERACTIONS WITH OTHER YOUTH, 3) ACT AS A ROLE MODEL, AND 4) SHARE THEIR EXPERIENCES WITH OTHER MONADNOCK OUTRIGHT REPRESENTATIVES TO IMPROVE THE ORGANIZATION.

1. Confidentiality is essential; at no time will any adult leader disclose the identities of any person involved with or in contact with Monadnock Outright, without specific consent from the individual, and the Board of Directors if the person is a youth, or except as required by law.

2. Adult facilitators are not crisis counselors; when a youth is in crisis or needs special help, adults should refer the youth for professional help. Therefore, adult leaders should familiarize themselves with the directory of resources that will be available at every youth meeting.

3. Adult facilitators should not establish and/or pursue a sexual or intimate relationship with any person under 22 years of age who utilizes any service or program of Monadnock Outright.

4. Youth meetings will not be held unless there are at least two adult facilitators present, one of whom will be a sexual minority whenever possible.

5. Youth are vulnerable to adults in positions of power; this may be especially true for lesbian, gay, bisexual, transgendered and questioning youth and their heterosexual allies. Therefore, Monadnock Outright does not encourage adult facilitators interacting with youth 1:1 outside youth meetings. If the adult feels it is necessary and/or appropriate to interact with youth outside of meetings, Monadnock Outright asks that volunteers not do so without another adult present. Remain aware of youths' vulnerability and act professionally.

6. When a situation arises where the appropriate course of action is unclear, the adult facilitator should consult with the Board of Directors before proceeding.

If action is needed before the next Board meeting, the volunteer should consult with at least two Board members (not including him/herself but including one of the Board chairs).

7. Adult volunteers should document and report to the Board Chairs or other Board member

a) any phone calls or contact with youth that is in any way related to significant family crisis, violence, physical or sexual abuse, suicide, runaway, harm to others, or other significant problems.

b) any situations involving another adult volunteer that appear to be unethical or dangerous to youth members.

8. All Monadnock Outright meetings where youth will be present are drug/alcohol-free environments. Please remember that adult volunteers are potential role models to youth, and representative of Monadnock Outright to community.

9. Adult volunteers wishing to spend their personal money on youth are urged to channel that money through Monadnock Outright in the form of a donation.

10. After each youth meeting, one of the facilitators will give a brief description of that evening's activities in the log book, including the names of all adult volunteers present and the number of youth attendees.

11. The Board of Directors of Monadnock Outright may terminate a volunteer's association with Monadnock Outright if it determines that the individual has blatantly violated any of the above stated policies and/or it determines, in its sole discretion, that such termination is in the best interest of Monadnock Outright.

I have read the above, understand it, and agree to abide by the above policies.

Signature_____ Date:_____

Print name_____

THESE ARE THE GUIDELINES FOR THE YOUTHS WHO ATTEND OUR MEETINGS:

Monadnock Outright exists in order to provide a safe space for gay, lesbian, transgender and questioning youth as well as their friends and allies to meet, share experiences, form friendships, and learn from one another. All youth ages fourteen to twenty-two are welcome to attend. We usually begin our meetings by going around and having each person tell how his/her week has gone, etc. Then we discuss anything people feel they need to go into more depth about, and then we usually socialize informally. On some occasions, we have speakers or films.

In order to help make the group work in everyone's best interest, we've set up the following guidelines for our meetings:

1. Respect Confidentiality. Confidentiality is something very important. It's not okay to share who was present or who said what. Also, if you see a group member outside the group in a public place, please use discretion. The member might not want his/her orientation revealed.

2. Meetings begin at seven o'clock. It is helpful if everyone arrives on time and doesn't leave until the end of each meeting. If you come in late or leave early while a group discussion is in progress, please do so without drawing attention to yourself (if at all possible.)

3. Inappropriate talk or discussion stifles discussion. Respect one another. If you disagree with a person's viewpoint, say so calmly and without judgment. Sexist, racist, homophobic, and other insensitive remarks are harmful. Please avoid talking over others or engaging in side talk. We need to learn to be sensitive and tolerant of each other. Appropriate (non-harmful) humor is encouraged; just remember that some members may want to be serious.

4. The use and/or possession of alcohol, drugs, and weapons is not permitted before and during the group. Those who smoke may do so outside the building and deposit cigarettes in a proper receptacle.

========================

Penny J. Culliton
2 Putnam Street #1
Wilton, NH 03086

APPENDIX 7:
PROJECTS & HINTS

Essay or Writing Contest

An essay or writing contest is an efficient and cost effective project to educate about GLBT issues. If the topic is carefully picked it can help create visibility and change attitudes.

One contest winner reported that just seeing the contest flyer posted on his high school bulletin board was an important and empowering event in his life. It is worth suggesting that the essay contest be offered as a required or extra credit assignment in appropriate classes.

The East Bay Chapter of BANGLE and now GLSEN San Francisco-East Bay have offered contests to high school students in its geographic area with the following topics:

1993 "A Gay Person I Admire"
1994 "A Coming Out Story"
1995 "A Gay Person I Admire" (Essay or interview.)
1997 "A Gay or Lesbian Role Model for Today's Youth"
1998 "Compare and Contrast GLBT Discrimination"*
  The discrimination and persecution that gay, lesbian, bisexual, and transgendered (GLBT) people face is sometimes compared to that based on race or religion at various points in history. Pick some specific area of persecution and discrimination in history and compare and contrast that to the persecution and discrimination faced by GLBT people today.
1999 "A GLBT Person That I Admire"
2000 "GLBT in the New Millennium" (Essay, short story, or poem.)

On the next page is the flyer used for the 1999 contest. Prizes of lower amounts, say $100, $50, and $25 could be used instead. I do strongly recommend using the phrase "Students retain copyright ownership of their entry, but by entering the contest grant..." as appears near the bottom of the flyer.

ESSAY CONTEST

"A GLBT* PERSON THAT I ADMIRE"

* GLBT is short for Gay, Lesbian, Bisexual, or Transgender

The essay may be about some famous contemporary or historical figure, or someone you know or interview.

First prize: $300   Second prize: $200   Third prize: $100

Sponsored by: **GLSEN/SF-EB**, Gay, Lesbian, and Straight Education Network/ San Francisco-East Bay (formerly BANGLE, Bay Area Network of Gay and Lesbian Educators)

• Essays must be **300-400 words** long, typed, double-spaced, and will be judged on how well they communicate information on the subject.

• The contest is open to **any high school student**, regardless of sexual orientation, in the counties of **San Francisco, Alameda, or Contra Costa**, in both public and private high schools. The contest is open to a high school student in **another area if the essay is submitted by a member of the San Francisco-East Bay chapter** of GLSEN.

• Be sure to include your name, grade, high school, and mailing address along with your essay. Please include a teacher's name if you use your school as your mailing address. Include a phone number if you would like to be notified by phone.

• Winners will be notified by May 1, 1999. The judging will be done by a panel of teachers and writers. Awards will be paid by check. In the case of ties, prize money will be split.

• No more than two entries may be submitted by a single student. Students retain copyright ownership of their entry, but by entering the contest grant GLSEN/SF-EB the right to publish the entry in the GLSTN/SF-EB newsletter.

• Entries must be postmarked by **Wednesday, March 31, 1999**.
Mail to: XXXXXXXXX

Conference Planning Hints

A conference is an excellent project. I had primary responsibility for one-day West Coast conferences in 1996 and 1997. Each had about 40 workshops with 400 people attending. I had no prior training. Based on my experiences here are some suggestions:

1. Arrange date and place ASAP (It would be good to be able to announce it a year in advance.)

2. Pick Title (Something that the radical right cannot easily attack.)
A subtitle could be "_____(your area) Conference on Gay, Lesbian, Bisexual, and Transgender Issues in Education."

3. Line up a keynote speaker. The better ones tend to be booked far into the future.

4. Decide on financing. (How profits or losses are shared.) Decide on conference fees. Sliding scale? Discount for early registration?
    Address to which registration fees will be sent.
    Phone number & e-mail address for information.

5. Issue press releases to Gay Press and over the internet with a call for presenters. (Major benefit: provides publicity for conference.)

6. Make a one-page flyer announcing the conference. (Distribute at Pride events, workshops, Film Festivals, etc.)

7. Contact previous and new presenters that you want to invite.
    Treat them like movie stars.

8. Establish Committees. The following are ones we used in 1996:
    Program
    Publications/Outreach
    Logistics
    Pre-registration
    On site registration
    Booths

9. Consult and involve ally organizations.

10. Consult and involve the organizations you are trying to educate, such as local school districts.

11. Get as much help as possible. Make sure that everyone understands what is expected. Include a means and schedule for regular accounting of accomplishments and problems.

APPENDIX 8:
WORKSHOP DESIGNS

Overview of a Half-Day Workshop for basic sexual orientation information that everyone should know. Suitable for faculty and administrators at all grade levels. This covers the same information that is suggested for "classes that teach sexuality," pages 8 and 9.

Session I. Introduction (30 minutes)

Welcome and Introductions
Get Acquainted Exercise (if needed)
Discussion Guidelines
Definitions
Quiz on Gay and Lesbian Issues

Session II. What We Know (60 minutes)

Human Sexuality/Kinsey Model
Research Tells Us
Historical Figures
Correlation of Suicide and Gay/Lesbian Conflict
Video: "Gay Youth."

Break (15 minutes)

Session III. Panel of Speakers (75 minutes)

Session IV. What We Need to Do (30 minutes)

The Project 10 Model
Teacher Resources
Student Resources
Evaluation

Interactive Workshop for Elementary School Teachers Using the Video "It's Elementary"

This workshop is designed for elementary school teachers who may have seen the 37-minute or TV version of "It's Elementary" and want to learn how to do similar units in their classes. The 78-minute version of "It's Elementary" will be viewed.

After viewing the video, each participant will be asked to choose a lesson and complete:
1. A Detailed Lesson Plan to include resources, discussion questions, supplies and materials, required authorizations (if any), etc.
2. A list of any concerns he or she may have about doing the lesson.
Each person or group will then do a presentation for the whole group.

It may be helpful to participants to have this list of the lessons as they watch the video:

1. PS 87, Public School, New York City.
   a. Cora Sangree, 4th grade teacher: Small group writing assignment: "What comes to mind when you hear: 'gay' or 'lesbian'?" Summarized on board. Whole group discussion: "Where do you get your ideas?"
   b. Scott Hirichfeld, 3rd grade teacher (end of film): Mother's Day, how celebrated, how do you define family. Emily, 3rd grade Guest Speaker reads her winning essay about her two Moms. Small group discussion on "Should gays be allowed to marry?"

2. Hawthorne Elementary, Public School, Madison, Wisconsin
   a. Daithi Wolfe, 3rd grade teacher: Make a web with "gay" in the center. Followed by (near end of film) discussion of famous gay and lesbian people using pictures, articles, music. (Both from history and current popular culture.)
   b. Kate Lyman, 1st/2nd grade teacher: Each student makes a page for a book, presents it to the class.
   c. Nancy Langdon, 5th grade teacher: Class discussion, pink triangles, put downs, etc.

3. Manhattan County School, Independent School, New York City. Carol 'Donnel, 8th grade English teacher: Write a 1-2 page paper on "gay- lesbian inclusion in the curriculum."
   Class discussion.

4. Peabody Elementary, Public School, Cambridge, Mass. Ellen Varella, Principal: Photo Text Exhibit: Love Makes a Family, viewed by one class at a time. Walter Davis, 5th grade teacher: discussion and answer questions after the viewing.

5. Luther Burbank Middle School, Public School, San Francisco, CA. Robert Roth, 8th grade Social Studies teacher: Cluster around "Stereotypes"; 10 minute writing assignment on
(1) Your own attitude towards homosexuality and
(2) What you would like to learn;
students volunteer to read aloud what they wrote.
Kim Coates, 8th grade Health Science teacher: (partly the same students) discussion.
Classes join for Guest Speakers (from Community United Against Violence) who tell a little about themselves and answer questions.
(In the film, we mostly get the questions asked, not answers.)
Follow up discussion: What was learned.

6. Cambridge Friends School, Quaker School, Cambridge, Mass. 4th Annual Gay Pride Day.
a. Thelma Delgado-Josey, 1st/2nd grade teacher: Read aloud *Asha's Moms* with discussion.
b. Helen McElroy, 3rd/4th grade teacher: Discussion: "Think of a word you heard that would be hurtful to a gay or lesbian person."
c. Thomas W. Price, Principal: Faculty meeting (the day before): "What are you going to do?", dealing with different faculty attitudes.
d. Assembly: Soccer playing gay teacher, songs.
e. Post assembly discussion for 6th, 7th, 8th grades.

(Notice that in the film we see mostly students talking, not teachers.)

After the video, allow about 30 minutes to make the lesson plan and list of concerns. Depending on group size, people might work alone or in small groups. Then begin presentations with feedback and suggestions.

Compile a list of concerns on the board. Brainstorm solutions. Each participant should pick a buddy and exchange phone numbers or e-mail addresses so they can provide each other support. Plan a future group meeting to discuss how it all went.

Possible time summary:

	Minutes
Introduction	12
Video "It's Elementary"	78
Break	10
Individual or Small Group Lesson Plan & List	30
Presentations of The Lesson	50
Break	10
Concerns List & Brainstorming	20
Buddy connections	10
Food & Drink (?)	
	210
	(3 1/2 hours)

APPENDIX 9:
COURT RULINGS

SUPREME COURT: SCHOOLS CANNOT IGNORE
SEXUAL HARASSMENT AMONG STUDENTS

Lesbian and gay kids often suffer from student-on-student sexual harassment.

The United States Supreme Court ruled Monday, May 24, 1999 that schools that willfully ignore sexual harassment of one student by another can be held liable for violating federal civil rights law. Lambda Legal Defense and Education Fund praised the 5-4 decision, noting that abuse of lesbian and gay students often involves sexual harassment from their peers.

Because Title IX, the federal law banning sex discrimination in public schools, is an important building block for creating safe and nurturing schools for all students, Lambda joined a friend-of-the-court brief in the case, which involves a Georgia fifth-grader who had been sexually harassed by a male student in her class.

Noting Nabozny vs. Podlesny, Lambda's successful constitutional lawsuit against a Wisconsin school district that ignored student brutality against a gay classmate, the federal government recently clarified that sexual harassment directed at lesbian and gay students is also covered by Title IX of the Education Amendments of 1972.

Lambda Legal Director Beatrice Dohrn said, "Sexual harassment of lesbian and gay students is a significant problem. The court has taken an important step in recognizing that school officials who turn a deaf ear to complaints of serious harassment and violence themselves facilitate the denial of educational opportunities to harassed students."

Lambda Staff Attorney David Buckel said, "Today's decision is very important to our struggle to make schools safe for lesbian and gay students, as violence and harassment by peers is the most common form these problems take."

"The High Court ruling sustains one of the many tools available to stop the harassment of lesbian and gay students," said Stephen R. Scarborough, staff attorney at Lambda's Southern Regional Office in Atlanta.

Writing for the majority in Davis v. Monroe County Board of Education, Justice Sandra Day O'Connor said lawsuits may be filed against school officials who knowingly and deliberately ignore student-on-student harassment.

The ruling remands the case to the district court, vacating an Eleventh Circuit U.S. Court of Appeals ruling that dismissed the lawsuit. The case was filed by Aurelia Davis, seeking damages after public school administrators in Monroe county, Georgia, ignored severe sexual harassment against her daughter LaShonda.

Referring to Title IX, O'Connor wrote, "The statute makes clear that, whatever else it prohibits, students must not be denied access to educational benefits and opportunities on the basis of gender."

Lambda, the nation's oldest and largest legal organization serving lesbians and gay men, joined an amicus brief authored by NOW Legal Defense and Education Fund. (Davis vs. Monroe County Board of Education, No. 97-843)

Website: www.lambdalegal.org

NEW JERSEY SUPREME COURT: BOY SCOUTS VIOLATED STATE ANTI-DISCRIMINATION LAW

(By Robert Hanley, New York Times, August 5, 1999)

TRENTON – Equating the Boy Scouts with such public accommodations as restaurants, libraries, schools and theaters, the New Jersey Supreme Court ruled Wednesday that the organization's expulsion of a gay Eagle Scout in 1990 violated the state's anti-discrimination law.

In a unanimous 7-to-0 decision, the court first rejected the Boy Scouts' arguments that it is a private organization and that its decision to remove the scout, James Dale, was protected by the First Amendment. The court also dismissed the Scouts' contention that homosexuality is immoral, comparing that view to discrimination against women and blacks.

After saying Mr. Dale's dismissal was "based on little more than prejudice," the Chief Justice, Deborah T. Poritz, wrote: "The sad truth is that excluded groups and individuals have been prevented from full participation in the social, economic and political life of our country.

The human price of this bigotry has been enormous.

At a most fundamental level, adherence to the principle of equality demands that our legal system protect the victim of invidious discrimination."

The case of Mr. Dale, who is now 29, is the second one to have reached the highest court in a state. But the result is just the opposite of the earlier case. In March 1998, the California Supreme Court ruled that the Scouts could expel homosexuals, agnostics and atheists.

That court held that the Boy Scouts were a private organization not covered by California's civil rights law and that the organization had constitutional rights of freedom of association and freedom of expression to expel homosexuals.

APPENDIX 10:
YOUTH SURVEY

Survey of Young GLBT People

A survey of Youth Groups at Pacific Center for Human Growth in Berkeley, California and at Lavender Youth Recreation and Information Center in San Francisco, California was made. A copy of the survey form is on the next page. The number of responses was small. However, based on discussions with other educators, I think the results accurately reflect the study group.

The survey results showed that the groups gave the **highest importance** to the following:

Δ Sexual orientation be included whenever diversity tolerance units are presented.

Δ Information on gay hotlines, groups, etc. be available to all students.

Δ Homosexuality be included whenever sexuality is taught.

Δ Teachers and staff do not let sexual orientation slurs go unchallenged.

Also important were the following:

Δ Teachers mention the sexual orientation of famous lesbians and gays when their contributions are covered.

Δ One or more counselors or teachers be designated as "Gay Sensitive" and willing to talk to students at each high school.

Δ English literature classes include one or more works that have lesbian or gay characters.

Δ Have a club for gay and lesbian students at school. (90% said they would have attended if a club had existed at their high school.)

Δ Gay Pride month be acknowledged at school.

Δ Teachers and staff who are lesbian or gay be "out" to students.

<u>Survey for "**The Invisible Minority--Meeting the Needs of Gay and Lesbian Youth**</u>", Richmond Unified School District Mentor Project
(Please return to Bob Latham, UTR GLC, xxxxx)

Age_____   Sex (M, F, TG) _____   Sexual Orientation (G, L, Bi)   _____

Date _____

The degree to which you were/are "out" in high school
(0 = to no one, 1 = to a few, 2 = to many, 3 = to everyone)   _____

The cities where your High Schools were/are located

_____

Please indicate the level of importance you attach to the following:
0 (No importance), 1, 2, 3, 4, 5 (Highest importance)

1. Teachers & staff do <u>not</u> let sexual orientation slurs go unchallenged_____

2. Teachers mention the sexual orientation of famous Lesbians and
Gays when their contributions are covered.   _____

3. Homosexuality be included whenever sexuality is taught.   _____

4. English literature classes include one or more works that have
Lesbian or Gay characters.   _____

5. Sexual orientation be included whenever diversity tolerance units
are presented.   _____

6. Gay Pride month be acknowledged at school.   _____

7. Information on Gay hotlines, groups, etc. be available to all students_____

8. One or more counselors or teachers be designated as "Gay Sensitive"
and willing to talk to students at each high school.   _____

9. Teachers and staff who are Lesbian or Gay be "out" to students.   _____

10. Have a club for Gay and Lesbian students at school.   _____

If such a club existed at your school, would you (have) attend(ed)?   _____

Comments, suggestions, ideas (please continue on the back of this page):

APPENDIX 11:
RECOMMENDED VIDEOS

All God's Children is an award-winning documentary chronicling the Black Church's acceptance of African American lesbians and gays. It is particularly good for students and faculties who object to discussing sexual orientation on religious grounds. It also helps correct the myth that homosexuality does not occur among people of color. (26 minutes, $29.95 individual/$69.95 institution)

Both My Moms' Names Are Judy is a provocative 10-minute video that shows elementary school children who have gay or lesbian parents talking about their experiences at school. The video is available from Lesbian & Gay Parents Association, 260, Tingley Street, San Francisco, CA 94112, Phone: 415-337-1629, e-mail: LGPASF@aol.com (10 minutes, $25 individual/$50 institution)

Gay Youth. This powerful video is extremely effective in showing why sexual orientation education is important. A variety of young people are interviewed, and the effect of family support is revealed. The results range from suicide to having a same-sex date for the senior prom. I have used this video for faculty at all grade levels as well as for high school students. Audiences always gave it high marks on the evaluation form. (40 minutes, $59.95)

It's Elementary: Talking About Gay Issues In Schools. This award winning video shows age appropriate lessons being taught in eight school districts across the country in grades kindergarten through eighth grade. It also shows why it is essential that information on sexual orientation be included at the elementary level. Two versions are available. The original 78-minute version is best for teachers who want to learn how to actually do the lessons. However there is a 37-minute excerpted version that may fit more easily into faculty meetings. "It's Elementary" was produced by Academy Award-Winner Debra Chasnoff and Helen Cohen of Women's Educational Media in San Francisco. (78 minutes: $99; 37 minutes: $75)

That's a Family! and **Let's Get Real** are also now available and **Stereotypes** is on the way. Visit Women's Educational Media's website, www.respectforall. org for detailed information about their outstanding videos.

Out of the Past traces the emergence of gay men and lesbians in American history through the eyes of a young woman coming to terms with herself. This film by Jeff Dupre won the Sundance Film Festival Audience Award for Best Documentary as well as a Bronze Apple from National Educational Media Foundation in 1998. (65 minutes, $25 individual/$99 institution)

Teaching Respect for All. In this video, Kevin Jennings, Executive Director and founder of GLSEN, presents a comprehensive training dealing with anti-gay bias in schools. Statistics are included to help parents, teachers, administrators and others to understand why schools must address anti-gay prejudice if all students--gay and straight--are to achieve their educational potential. (52 minutes, $49.95)

APPENDIX 12:
RECOMMENDED BOOKS

HIGH SCHOOL/MIDDLE SCHOOL LEVEL &
GENERAL BACKGROUND:

("BANGLE Books" are preceded by * .One or two copies of each book was donated to all the public high schools in California's Contra Costa County during 1992-93 by BANGLE, Bay Area Network of Gay and Lesbian Educators. Books preceded by ~ were recommended by Kate Evans.)

Aarons, Leroy. ***Prayers for Bobby, A Mother's Coming to Terms with the Suicide of Her Gay Son***. *Prayers for Bobby* is a must-read for any parent or educator who is involved in a situation where religion and sexual orientation are at odds. It chronicles the heartbreaking life of Bobby Griffith. What make this book so poignant are the excerpts from Bobby's journals. He began writing a few months before coming out to his brother in the spring of 1979, shortly before his sixteenth birthday. His journal gives a rare insight of the turmoil queer youth suffer. The deep self-loathing and pain draw the reader into a world rarely seen by straights. The root of Bobby's self-hatred was his Christian fundamentalist upbringing. His deeply devout mother instilled the traditional Protestant fear of God. Upon learning of her son's gayness, she began a battle to save Bobby's soul. With all her heart she believed Bobby would be cured of this disease through prayer. After his suicide, Bobby's mother, Mary Griffith, became a strong spokesperson for queer youth.

Bagemihl, Bruce. ***Biological Exuberance: Animal Homosexuality and Natural Diversity***. Saint Martin's Press. New York. 1999. This book by a Ph.D. biologist and researcher has over 700 pages of documented information that fulfills the promise of the title. It would be a worthwhile addition to all high school libraries and biology teacher's desks.

~ Bass, Ellen and Kate Kaufman. ***Free Your Mind: The Book for Gay, Lesbian, and Bisexual Youth and Their Allies***. HarperPerennial. New York. 1996. A beautifully written look at self-discovery, friends and lovers, family, school, spirituality, and community for lesbian, gay, and bisexual teens, as well as their parents, teachers and friends. Chock-full of inspiring quotes, narrative accounts, biographical sketches of famous lesbians and gay men, and marvelous photographs, this book is an empowering must-have.

~ Bauer, Marion Dane (Ed.). *Am I Blue? Coming Out from the Silence*. HarperTrophy. New York. 1994. An award-winning short-story anthology compiling varied approaches to lesbian and gay lives, from teenagers coming out to themselves, to straight teenagers with a gay parent, friend, or sibling. The title story, "Am I Blue," by Bruce Coville is replete with witty characterizations, humor, and poignancy. Other included writers read like a "Who's Who" of Young Adult literature, with M.E. Kerr, Francesca Lia Block, Nancy Garden, Leslea Newman, and Lois Lowry.

~ Block, Francesca Lia. (1995). *Baby Be-Bop*. New York: HarperTrophy. Popular, good-looking, surfer-boy Dirk McDonald transforms into a leather-jacketed, mohawked slam-dancer once it is clear his love for his best friend will never be reciprocated. The inner turmoil and agony of coming out to himself leads Dirk to dangerous places where swastika-tattooed skinheads beat up "faggots." After a graphically-depicted beating, Dirk lapses into a swirling series of stories from his past, magically relayed through people long-dead. Chock-full of sensory-rich description, Block's story conveys a dream-like, fairy tale-esque tone in conjunction with a realistic portrayal of the shocking manifestations of (self-) hatred.

* Borhek, Mary V. *Coming Out to Parents*. The Pilgrim press. Cleveland. 1983. This book was written by a parent with chapters for parents as well as lesbians and gay men. It gives an excellent introduction to homosexuality as well as practical advice in family communication. It includes a chapter on religious issues that stands alone and should be read by anyone with concerns in that area.

* Brett, Catherine. *S.P. Likes A.D.* The Women's Press. Toronto. 1989. This is a short book (119 pages) with an easy reading level. The main character is a young women coming to terms with an attraction to a female classmate. She never tells the classmate. Supporting characters include an older lesbian couple.

* Cowan, Thomas. *Gay Men and Women Who Enriched the World*. Alyson Publications, Inc. 1992. This book gives short biographies of forty famous people who have made significant contribution and who are gay. This book is highly recommended both for student and teacher use.

Druker, Peter. ***Different Rainbows***. Millivres Ltd. 2000. Different Rainbows is an impressive and pioneering collection of essays on lesbian and gay movements in the Third World. Ten authors provide information about Mexico, Brazil, Latin America, Nicaragua, Africa, India, Kenya, and China. Some of the essays are insightful and intellectually stimulating. As well as providing a better understanding of the Third World and diverse people you may meet anywhere, the book leads to a clearer understanding of all of GLBT history. A sample insight: Identity may be separate from activity. Some languages have a verb for activity but not a noun for a gay or lesbian or homosexual person.

* Duberman, ed. Martin. ***Hidden from History: Reclaiming the Gay & Lesbian Past***. Penguin Books. New York. 1989. This book is a scholarly look at gay history (579 pages.) Included are sections on the ancient world, pre-industrial societies, the nineteenth century, early twentieth century, and World War II and the postwar era. This is a good reference book for teachers, but the Cowan book above is probably better for general student use.

* Flagg, Fannie. ***Fried Green Tomatoes/Whistle Stop Cafe***. McGraw-Hill, Inc. New York. 1988. This best seller would be an excellent book to use in English classes along with the academy award caliber movie based on it (Jessica Tandy was nominated for best supporting actress.) The book incorporates an interesting style of writing. It has many short chapters set in different time periods. The Lesbian relationship is more developed in the book than in the movie. The relationship is presented in a low-key, tasteful manner.

* Griffin, Carolyn; Wirth, Marian; Wirth, Arthur. ***Beyond Acceptance***. St. Martin's Press. New York. 1986. Parents of Lesbians and Gays talk about their experiences in this excellent book (199 pages.) Quotes from many interviews with lesbians, gays, and their parents are included. Highly recommended for everyone.

Hartinger, Brent. ***Geography Club***. HarperCollins Publishers Inc. New York. 2003. This is a short, easy-read novel with lots of contemporary teenage dialog that quickly captures reader interest. Gay high school students discover each other and decide to form a Geography Club in order to get together without drawing attention to themselves. Highly recommended for everyone, especially teenagers.

* Huber, PhD, Jeffrey T. *How to Find Information about AIDS, 2nd Ed*. Harriington Park Press, Inc. New York. 1992. This book lists of all types of organizations with addresses and phone numbers that have anything to do with AIDS (288 pages.) Nothing about sexual orientation is included except that some of the organizations have gay or lesbian in their titles.

~ Jennings, Kevin. *Becoming Visible: A Reader in Gay and Lesbian History for High School and College Students*. Alyson Publications. Boston. 1994. A compilation of varied voices that walk students through Greco-Roman conceptions of homosexuality, to the "homophile" movement of the 1950's, to Stonewall, to Bowers v. Hardwick. Cogent introductions to each chapter make for a seamless read. Each chapter includes follow-up questions and thought-provoking activities.

Kay, Phillip and Andrea Espepa and Al Desetta (Editors.) *Out With It: Gay and Straight Teens Write About Homosexuality*. Youth Communications. New York. 1996. Chapter titles include That Gay Thing, Friends and Family, Coming Out, Homophobia, Gender Benders, Looking Back, and Resources for Teachers. Many pieces would be ideal to copy for classroom use (which is encouraged by reprint permission and format).

~ Kerr, M.E. *Deliver Us From Evie*. New York. HarperTrophy. 1994. Most people in this small town in rural Missouri accept seventeen-year-old Evie's penchant for short hair and "manly" dress--that is until she and beautiful Patsy Duff fall in love. Parr Burrman, Evie's brother, must process not only his own reactions and those of his family, but his own girlfriend's beliefs that homosexuality is a sin.

* Miller, Isabel. *Patience & Sarah*. Fawcett Crest. New York. 1969. A historical novel set in nineteenth century New England (192 pages.) A good choice to illustrate point of view in writing classes. The narration alternates between Patience and Sarah as their story unfolds. A Literary Guild selection.

* Perry, Reverend Troy; Swigegood, Thomas. *Profiles in Gay & Lesbian Courage*. St. Martin's Press. New York. 1991. The stories of eight gay figures that showed bravery, dignity, and true courage are told in an engaging, even compelling way. Included are Harvey Milk, Elaine Noble, Gilberto Gerald, Jean O'Leary, Leonard Matlovich, Barbara Gittings, Harry Hay, and Ivy Bottini.

~ Price, Deb and Joyce Murdoch. *And Say Hi to Joyce: America's First Gay Column Comes Out*. Doubleday. New York. 1995. In her pithy, compressed style, Deb Price (the first out-lesbian nationally-syndicated columnist) addresses an array of political and personal topics. Price's writings are interspersed with chapters by her partner, Joyce Murdoch, detailing the bumpy, poignant, and often funny travails of their public and private lives.

* Rafkin, Louise. *Different Daughters*. Cleis Press. San Francisco. 1987. Twenty-five mothers talk about the growth of their relationships with their lesbian daughters.

* Rafkin, Louise. *Different Mothers*. Cleis Press. San Francisco. 1990. Twenty eight children (age five to forty) talk about growing up in lesbian families.

Read, Kirk. *How I learned to Snap*. Hill Street Press LLC. 2001. This book includes over 50 vignettes that manage to fill his "small-town coming-of-age and coming-out story" with unique and interesting details while also providing universal connections to all of us. It was nominated for a 2001 Lambda Award. Read grew up in the South and was precocious in many areas including drinking, sex, and writing as well as snapping. While in high school he won an award for writing a play about coming out in high school.

Renault, Mary. *The Last of the Wine*. Pocket Books, Inc. New York. 1964. This is an excellent historical novel set in ancient Greece during the wars between Athens and Sparta. Mary Renault brings the era alive while including many carefully researched historic facts including gay relationships. This novel is one of my personal favorites.

* Sakers, Don. *Lucky in Love*. Alyson Publications, Inc. Boston. 1987. A good novel in which the teenage narrator falls in love with a classmate who is the star of the basketball team (175 pages.) Theirs is an interracial as well as a gay relationship. The romance and sexual aspects are particularly well done in that they manage to be positive and present without being explicit or objectionable.

* Scoppettone, Sandra. *Trying Hard to Hear You*. Alyson Publications, Inc. Boston. 1991. Excellent novel that I found difficult to put down. (264 pages.) The story is set in a close-knit teenage summer theater group. Unusual depth and complex plot threads make this a novel to consider using in English classes. The fact that two members of the group are gay is not disclosed until the second

half of the book. First person narration is by a straight sixteen-year-old. Sexual orientation is only one of several facets of the story. Highly recommended.

~ Singer, Bennet L. (Ed). New Press. New York. 1993. ***Growing Up Gay/ Growing Up Lesbian: A Literary Anthology***. An anthology of stories, poems, and essays by such writers as Rita Mae Brown, Jeanette Winterston, and James Baldwin.

* Valez, Jr., Ivan. ***Tales of the Closet, #1-7***. Hetrick-Martin Institute, Inc. New York. 1987 to 1992. This is a sequence of seven graphic books bound together. They are published by The Hetrick-Martin Institute, Inc. founded by Emery S. Hetrick, M.D., a psychiatrist, and A. Damien Martin, Ed.D., a New York University professor. The books cover the topics of isolation, family, violence, health, pregnancy, religion, and stress all in a responsible, effective, and entertaining way.

~ Van Dijk, Lutz. ***Damned Strong Love***. (Elizabeth D. Crawford, Trans.). Henry Holt and Company. New York. 1995. (Original work published in1991). Based on a true story, this novel set during World War II chronicles the love between Stefan, a Polish teenager, and Willi, a German soldier. Their love is damned not only because they are gay during a time and place when same-sex love could be punished by imprisonment and even death, but because they love across opposite sides of the war. The book smoothly incorporates a tense, action-filled story with bittersweet personal moments and historical information.

Warren, Patricia Nell. ***Billy's Boy***. Wildcat Press. Beverly Hills. 1997. This is the third novel in the series that began with ***The Front Runner***. The narrator in this novel is a teenage boy who searches for information about the mysterious death of his gay father and eventually learns that his mother is a lesbian. The novel covers all of the issues that GLBTQ youth sometimes face in schools and in society in an interesting way and should appeal to high school students.

~ Woodson, Jacqueline. ***From the Notebooks of Melanin Sun***. Scholastic. New York. 1995. This beautifully written novel explores the inner life of Melanin Sun, a gifted thirteen-year-old whose world is shaken when his mother falls in love another woman--and a white woman, at that. Throughout the novel, Woodson weaves themes of difference and "fitting in" in relationship to racial and sexual identity, as well as subtlety probing the notion that confusion about oneself lies at the center of prejudice. $5.99 list price in paper back.

Yates, Bart. *Leave Myself Behind*. Kensington Books. Leave Myself Behind is an engrossing coming-out novel. The first chapter may be read at http://www. kensingtonbooks.com (At the site, type in the title, Leave Myself Behind, and click on Go.)

MIDDLE SCHOOL & ELEMENTARY:

Abramchik, Lois, illustrated by Alaiyo Bradshaw, edited by Barbara L. Cavallo. *Is Your Family Like Mine?* Open Heart, Open Mind. New York. 1993. Armetha has a Mom and a Mommy who answer her quesion "How come I don't have a Daddy?" The illustrations include classmates of various racial backgrounds. Ages 6-12. $10. To order or request information call 718-788-5146.

Bauer, Marion Dane. *Am I Blue? Coming Out From the Silence*. 1994. 16 original short stories, each by a noted author. An honest portrayal of growing up gay or lesbian or having gay or lesbian parents. Ages 12 and up. 273 pages. $5.95.

Elwin, Rosamund and Michele Paulse. *Asha's Mums*. 1990. As featured in the video "It's Elementary," confusion erupts when Asha brings back a permission form signed by both her moms. Ages 5 and up. 28 pages. $4.95.

Garden, Nancy, illustrated by Sharon Wooding. *Molly's Family*. 2004. In this picture book, kindergartner Molly makes a drawing for Open School Night that includes her two mamas which causes questions from her a classmate. Molly's conversations with her two mothers and support from her teacher leads to recognition and celebration of family diversity. 32 pages. $16.00

Heron, Ann and Meredith Maran. *How Would You Feel If Your Dad Was Gay?* 1991. Jasmine, Michael, and Noah are all regular kids except for one thing--Jasmine and Michael have two gay fathers and Noah has a lesbian mother. A fictional tale from the hearts and minds of children. Ages 6-12. 47 pages. $6.95.

Kennedy, Joseph and John Canemaker. *Lucy Goes to the Country*. 1998. Lucy is a little cat who travels from her city apartment to the countryside for an adventure-filled weekend with her two Big Guys, family, and friends. Oversize hardcover, pictures. Ages 2 and up. 32 pages. $15.95.

Scholastic. *The Crayon Box That Talked*. 1998. Written as a poem, this is a story about a little girl who discovers a box of talking crayons, all complaining about each other. It provides an excellent way to introduce diversity to young students. Ages 2 and up. $1.95 from Scholastic, 800-724-2424.

Skutch, Robert, illustrations by Laura Niemnaus. *Who's in a Family?* 1995. Addresses the many different kinds of families in which people live, including gay and lesbian, single parent, and multiracial. Ages 3-6. 29 pages. $6.95.

Valentine, Johnny. *One Dad Two Dads, Brown Dad Blue Dads*. 1994. In a fun and easy-to-read story, two children compare notes about their different families, who in the end aren't really all that different. Hardcover. 29 pages. $10.95.

Vigna, Jesica. *My Two Uncles*. 1995. This illustrated book for young children explores family reactions to homosexuality and demonstrates the importance of intergenerational communication and understanding.

Woodson, Jacqueline. *From The Notebooks of Melanin Sun*. See High School/Middle School section above. Ages 12 and up. $5.99.

ABOUT THE AUTHOR:

Bob Latham taught high school chemistry and physics for 27 years and has been a part-time field supervisor for a university education department, mentoring intern teachers, for 10 years. He has been involved in working for GLBT rights during his career in education including

1. Doing a Mentor Project titled "The Invisible Minority—Meeting the Needs of Gay and Lesbian Youth" (1993-94).

2. Starting a Gay & Lesbian Caucus in his teacher union, which obtained Domestic Partner Health Benefits.

3. Initiating the National Education Association resolution on sexual orientation, which was passed in 1994 and 1995.

4. Organizing West Coast Conferences on GLBT Issues in Education in 1995 and 1996.

5. Acting as Volunteer Executive Director for BANGLE and GLSEN SF-EB, 1996 to 1999.

Bob Latham was born in California in 1939, attended Stanford University on scholarships, worked as a chemical engineer for DuPont, got a MChE degree from the University of Delaware, and worked for Chevron before switching into teaching. He designed and built a house in Point Richmond and retired early to study creative writing and work as a volunteer for GLBT organizations. Bob Latham had three long-term relationships: Marriage at age 20 to Linda (15 years, two children, divorced), then Stan (15 years, sudden death), and finally Alex (13 years, 7,000 miles apart). Many details of his unusual life are disclosed in *Boysenberry Pie: A Memoir of Vignettes*, published in 2004.

Bob Latham continues to edit a free monthly GLBT literary zine which is posted at www.Q-zine.com. The zine began in July 2001 and the website includes back issues.

In 2004, just as *Boysenberry Pie* came out, Bob Latham was diagnosed as having Amyotrophic Lateral Sclerosis (ALS), also commonly called Lou Gehrig's disease. He is now (to use his words) a guinea pig for ALS research.